Team Teaching

Organization and Administration

Leslie J. Chamberlin
Bowling Green State University

Charles E. Merrill Publishing Company
A Bell & Howell Company
Columbus, Ohio

To John Rufi

A teacher who expected his students to study.

A friend loyal to those he taught.

Standard Book Number: 675-09520-4

Library of Congress Card Number: 69-14633

1 2 3 4 5 6 7 8 9 10 / 73 72 71 70 69

Printed in the United States of America

Preface

The current surge to make use of team teaching organization has increased educational opportunities. More and more schools across our country are beginning to use this new organizational plan, perhaps because team teaching is one of the most imaginative and flexible approaches to improving the teaching-learning situation to be tried in this half of the 20th century. Many educators hope that it will prove to be the vehicle for bringing about long overdue changes in American education.

Team teaching is still in the developmental stages. Patterns vary and much experimentation continues. However, enough of the theoretical potential of team teaching has been demonstrated to justify the current interest in it. But this variety of patterns is often confusing, and some educators wonder how an appropriate approach to team teaching can be arranged. This book is a compact presentation of the points most necessary for a basic understanding of team teaching and the successful adoption of a team teaching program.

Team Teaching Organization and Administration attempts to apply team teaching theory to the everyday classroom situation. It offers a practical approach to beginning and operating a team teaching program. The guide lines presented are directed toward the professional and nonprofessional personnel who have the responsibility for administering the daily program. It is a manual of theory and practice; it emphasizes *why* and *how*.

Other purposes of this book are to acquaint its readers with the evolving concept of team teaching; to provide an analysis of the major dimensions of team teaching; and to stimulate critical assessment of the team teaching idea. A compact, simple presentation has been achieved through extensive use of the Breve technique. The reader is encouraged to study each Breve carefully.

It is hoped that undergraduates enrolled in "method" education courses, graduate students studying educational supervision and/or administration, as well as both beginning and experienced professional personnel planning a team teaching program will find this book both interesting and helpful.

In an attempt to present a true picture of team teaching, some of the plans, procedures and comments of teachers and administrators currently using team teaching in actual school situations have been obtained by personal interview and questionnaire and are reported in some detail. Grateful acknowledgement is made for this assistance as well as for the many ideas contributed by colleagues, consultants, and teachers and students in the field. Thanks is also expressed to my family, especially my daughter and typist, Linda, who demonstrated true team spirit during the writing of this text.

LJC

Picture Credits

Photographs on pages 94, 95, 101, and 102 reproduced with permission from Perkins and Will Partnership Architects. Photographs on pages 26, 32, 44, 67, 68, 69, and 110 from *The Kent State University School: A Laboratory School in Action,* edited by Parker LaBach, photographs by Doug Moore, Kent State University staff photographer, and reproduced with permission from Kent State University. Photograph on page 46 reproduced with permission of Sylvania City Schools, Sylvania, Ohio.

Contents

THE BREVE

A unique and original feature of this publication is the "Breve." Use of this technique allows the text to move quickly since the more detailed and/or complicated information and ideas are in a related but separate presentation. The Breve is not a summation. Each Breve represents an attempt by the author to present important information in a condensed or abridged form. The Breve technique also creates for the student a concise, organized aid to study.

The Breves

The Breves (Con't.)

part
one

Basic
Understandings

Focus on the Individual

1

Team Teaching—Why?

Socio-Cultural and Technical Factors

This country's educational programs are merely an extension of the social-cultural goals of our total society. The goals of the public schools are subject to the constant pressure of our social and cultural forces. However, this relationship between the social system and the education system is not a direct one. There was a time when a lag of as much as fifty years passed between the invention of a new technique or material and the adoption of it by the schools. Today this time lag is perhaps as brief as five years under certain conditions. One technique which is being adopted this quickly is team teaching.

Important social and cultural factors which are too powerful to be held in abeyance are today pressuring for an examination of, and perhaps changes in, traditional teacher behavior and school organizational patterns. Present knowledge of how children learn, grow, and develop seems to be in conflict with certain patterns of educational organization. A sense of urgency in the process of educational change has been caused by many factors including the explosive increase in knowledge, the creation of new kinds of occupations, the mobility

BREVE 1

New Technical Developments

Rateometer (Photo Courtesy of Audio-Visual Research).

Filmstrip Projector

of our modern population, the immigration to the metropolitan areas, and the deterioration of inner-cities, combined with the impact of science and technology on education, and the ideological conflict in which this country is involved. Breve 1 illustrates the application of two of the many new teaching aids being used in the schools. The rate of educational change is being hastened by the movement of modern technical developments into the schools.

Teaching tasks must also change because of these social, cultural, and technological developments. Just as past teaching techniques have been changed, better approaches to teaching which satisfy current problems must now be developed. The wide range of individual differences which exist in the various populations served by the schools of this nation must be acknowledged and provided for through instructional organization. Teachers who know how to make adequate provisions for the extreme ranges of individual differences found in pupil populations are in short supply. Therefore, ways must be developed to provide quality educational programs which meet the needs of the individual student.

Too long have the educational systems of this country used the lock-step approach to education which is based on such false assumptions as:

1. Students learn at the same rate.

2. The same curriculum content is appropriate for all students.

3. A pupil-teacher ratio of 30/1 is *the* appropriate group size.

4. Periods of equal length are appropriate for all learning activities.

5. The self-contained classroom can provide adequate learning opportunities for the modern world.

At the present, most of the schools of this nation continue to use the traditional method of one teacher teaching one subject at a time. In the elementary school, the teacher normally allots enough time during the day to present each subject to her class. The high school teacher usually teaches one subject to various groups of students. Some new innovations have been tried, but the majority of our instructional patterns still follow the traditional one-teacher, one-subject, read, recite and recall process.

Many educators believe that the self-contained classroom will not fully utilize the current developments in educational technology and that it cannot completely satisfy the need for greater individualization of instruction. Nationally, there have been several attempts to change from the self-contained classroom concept to some organizational pattern that is more efficient both educationally and economically. Perhaps the most educationally effective teaching situation would be a one teacher—one pupil ratio; however, this pattern would obviously not be workable because of the financial and human support it would require. Nevertheless, providing individual attention is a desirable goal, and there are efforts to achieve it in the instructional organizations being investigated. In *Schools for the Sixties* the National Education Association states that in order to provide individually planned programs for learners which permit flexibility in assigning pupils to groups that may range in size from one pupil to as many as a hundred or more, well-planned cooperative efforts among teachers, such as team teaching, should be encouraged and tested.

To capitalize on the most efficient use of teachers in terms of their backgrounds, subject area specialization, and interests, many organizational patterns that would seem to fit under the general name *team*

BREVE 2

Why Team Teaching?

Selected Reasons

- Curriculum explosion and demand for more knowledgeable teachers
- Demand for better staff utilization
- Demand for improvement in quality of education
- Larger enrollments
- More diversified student populations
- More sophisticated instructional media resulting from impact of science and technology
- Need for flexibility in instructional organization to provide greater variety of educational experiences
- Need for greater individualization
- Belief that teachers are more effective when working as group members
- Belief that team teaching is more efficient educationally

teaching are being explored. Several reasons for the current extensive study of team teaching are listed in Breve 2. Due to the high public interest in education, the increased availability of money for educational research, and the pressing challenges of the future, we can expect more and greater interest in this innovative approach to instructional organization.

Advantages of Team Teaching

Promoters of the team approach to teaching claim many advantages for this new technique. As Breves 3 through 7 indicate, the advantages begin to appear in the planning stages and become even more obvious in the team teaching program itself. However, the main strength of the team approach seems to be in its flexible as well as controlled use of physical facilities and teacher talents.

Team teaching does demand that all cooperating teachers have common objectives; however, one significant advantage of this structure is that the teachers can pool their creative ideas, knowledge, and talent to meet these objectives and thus provide better instruction for the students. In fact each team member stimulates the others, producing a spiral development of both content and method ideas for the enrichment of the instructional program.*

BREVE 3

Team Teaching Advantages

Planning Stage

- Opportunity to redefine goals of education
- Opportunity for in-service instruction
- Opportunity to reorganize instructional patterns
- Opportunity to stimulate community interest

In addition to improving the program, team teaching also encourages growth by team members through their close associations with fellow

---

*Stanley L. Freeman, "The Growth-Learning Process," 3rd Annual Report to the Ford Foundation on Team Teaching, University of Maine, 1965, p. 7.

BREVE 4

Team Teaching Advantages
The Student

- Pupils become more independent under team teaching
- The team concept can help to build a sense of responsibility in the students
- The team approach provides flexibility to meet the varying needs of the several school populations
- Pupils can be grouped in areas of special interest to them
- Student-teacher personality problems can be reduced
- Superior teachers are shared by all students
- The team approach permits greater attention to individual students
- Team teaching can provide for improved guidance activities

team members. One location of such growth is in the respective specialties of the participating members. The collective abilities, knowledge, and experience of all team members are utilized in planning, and the judgment and contributions of each member can be applied and evaluated. Such activity creates wonderful in-service training opportunities, since each teacher can learn from the specialized talents of his team colleagues. Team members also learn from each other by thinking, planning, differing, making decisions, and teaching together.

Team teaching can solve another problem, too. In a keynote address to the 1968 Ohio Elementary School Principals Professional Conference, Braulio Alonso, while president of the National Education Association, reported that recent NEA research revealed that one of the most frequent complaints voiced by teachers is that they are not given time to teach. Lunchroom, playground, and other supervisory responsibilities, combined with collecting money and clerical duties, demand much of their time. Team teaching enables a teacher to utilize his time in a more professional manner since aides are often used to perform the majority of non-instructional tasks.

Members of a teaching team can experience interest, excitement, and satisfaction as a result of substituting an individual-based organ-

BREVE 5

Team Teaching Advantages
Staff

- Differentiates but does not detract from teacher role
- Encourages able teachers to remain in the classroom
- Increases opportunity for personal recognition
- Makes more effective use of the professional talents and interests of staff members
- Relieves teachers of routine tasks through the use of aides
- Enables teachers to share information and ideas which help solve problems and improve their professional background
- Encourages each member to do his very best
- Results in lower pupil-staff ratio
- Reduces the adverse results of teacher absence
- Neutralizes the effect of the poor teacher
- Provides in-service education opportunities

ization for a rigid grade-placement organization, providing greater opportunity for learners to engage in individual and small group projects, using programed teaching materials, releasing teachers from managerial assignments by utilizing the services of teacher aides, and participating in professional study and planning with fellow team members.

Possible Limitations

Perhaps a chapter entitled "Team Teaching—Why?" is an odd place to present a list of the problems sometimes connected with team teaching, but this is done in the interest of providing the reader with both the pros and cons at the outset of his study of team teaching.

High on the list of difficulties inherent in team teaching is the problem of the human equation. It seems that some teachers find it difficult to work cooperatively and on a professional level with their peers. Breve 8 shows other limitations sometimes encountered.

BREVE 6

Team Teaching Advantages

Teaching-Learning Situation

- Allows students to work across grade lines with subject matter specialists
- Allows better control of pupil-staff ratio through use of large, medium and small grouping
- Provides children with several adult images to study
- Improves correlation of school work, home work, and field experiences
- Makes for a more balanced curriculum
- Provides for flexible scheduling
- Provides a wider range of grouping possibilities
- Provides a wider resource of talent, knowledge, skills, and experience from which to derive new educative experiences
- Gives teachers an opportunity to set examples of cooperation and sharing
- Takes advantage of the fact that the "whole" of the participants working together will be more than the "sum" of the individual staff members working independently

BREVE 7

Team Teaching Advantages

Facilities & Equipment

- School facilities can be used more efficiently
- Team instruction encourages fuller utilization of audio-visual and other instructional media
- Team teaching provides an opportunity for classroom experimentation in instructional media

BREVE 8

Team Teaching Limitations

■ Agreement on the evaluation of individual students

■ Arranging time for planning, instructional development, and study during the day

■ Increased pressure on students resulting from constant upgrading of instruction

■ Conflicts resulting from mixing people of different teaching styles

■ Providing facilities capable of furnishing the flexibility needed

■ Replacing teachers who leave the team

■ Requests for additional audio-visual materials and equipment resulting from team-teaching organization

■ Selection of appropriate action regarding student misbehavior

■ Teacher insecurity, dread of the unfamiliar often accompany beginning team teaching

■ The need for a designated leader

■ The question of more pay for team leaders

■ Danger of pupil detachment with the use of large groups

■ Tendency to restrict the individual teacher's freedom of action

The success of a team teaching program seems to depend more on the willingness of the staff to plan and work together than on the details of structure. Communication, cooperation, and collaboration seem to be the important "three C's" of team teaching. Therefore, selecting the staff may be a problem. Also, providing time for joint planning sessions seems to be an obstacle.

Although the danger of pupil detachment is sometimes mentioned as a result of large-group instruction, this can be overcome through proper planning. A feeling of team camaraderie can be developed by demonstrating to the students that they are accepted as individuals of worth and that their ideas, goals, and feelings are important. A carefully planned orientation and motivation program is very important in creating this feeling. One of the more pleasant outcomes that can be derived from a team organization is a closer pupil-staff relationship.

Evaluations of Team Teaching

There is a dearth of genuine research on team teaching. An assessment by Judson Shaplin of Washington University indicates why this is so. He states that team teaching too prevalently is described in highly general terms. Also, all projects have become experiments, and objectives are often stated as hypotheses. In fact, many projects are merely educational demonstrations of preferred practices with few of the variables identified, much less controlled, in any experimental sense. The hypotheses are usually stated in such general terms that it is impossible to establish conditions under which statistics can be derived.*

Brownell and Taylor, after five to six years of functional experience with team teaching, recommend closer analysis of assumptions, more explicit models, better research design, and more penetrating evaluation of results so that educators will be able to make sound judgments about teaching teams.†

Robert H. Anderson worked for four years with the original pioneer team teaching project at the Franklin School of Lexington, Massachusetts. Under the auspices of Harvard's SUPRAD (School and University Program for Research and Development), he concluded that the team teaching results are no less satisfactory than the results of typical teaching situations. In addition, team teaching appears to be especially beneficial to the very advanced and retarded pupils.‡

The Dundee School, Greenwich, Connecticut, underwent a two-year evaluation which was headed by Willard Elsbree of the Teachers College, Columbia University. The results were released in February, 1965. In the area of academic achievement, the report indicated that no conclusive evidence could be found to suggest that standardized achievement test scores are improved or decreased as a result of team teaching. However, in other areas of student achievement the report indicated that when compared to control pupils, Dundee students seemed to mention more frequently the social aspects of school life, tended to depend more on peers than adults for assistance, and generally scored higher in fluency and flexibility on the Minnesota Tests of Creative Thinking.

---

*Judson T. Shaplin and Henry F. Olds, Jr. (eds.), *Team Teaching*, New York: Harper and Row, (1964), p. 7.

†John A. Brownell and Harris A. Taylor, "Theoretical Perspectives for Teaching Teams," *Phi Delta Kappan*, XLIII (January 1962), p. 157.

‡Robert H. Anderson, "Team Teaching," *NEA Journal*, Vol. L (March 1961), p. 54.

An emerging syntheses regarding team teaching is that it is accomplishing the general objectives of teaching at least as effectively as the more traditional plans. The essential assets seem to be a highly flexible base for grouping and a better utilization of teacher strengths. No one claims team teaching to be a panacea, but neither have been the various plans associated with the one-teacher control or self-contained classroom concepts. It seems that the evaluation of team teaching will, for years to come, depend almost entirely on educational theory and subjective experience since the variables of team teaching are almost innumerable and difficult to control in any conclusive research attempt. These remarks are not intended to discourage research in this area, but only to reduce future research expectations to more realistic proportions.

But our schools and instructional practices must change to meet the needs of today's youth. Perhaps Dean and Witherspoon hit upon the most important value of the team teaching movement in this statement: "Inherent in the [team teaching] plan is an increased degree of flexibility for teacher responsibility, grouping policies and practices, and size of groups, and *an invigorating spirit of freedom and opportunity to revamp programs to meet the educational needs of children.*"*

---

*Stuart E. Dean and Clinette F. Witherspoon, "Team Teaching in the Elementary Schools," *Education Briefs*, OE-23022, Washington, D.C.: U.S. Department of Health, Education, and Welfare, (1962), p. 4.

2

Team Teaching—What?

A Definition

Team teaching is a difficult concept to define. In recent years considerable interest has centered upon organizational schemes which permit greater flexibility in the grouping of students and the utilization of teachers. Different terms have become attached to certain plans, but the majority of them can be classified under the name *team teaching*. However, a survey by the author of sixty-eight schools in seventeen states which were known to be using an innovative school organization indicated that team teaching programs vary a great deal. In fact team teaching seems to be an "umbrella" term which is used to describe a large number of innovative instructional organizations. Under the title of team teaching one finds programs which range from some simple form of cooperative planning to a relatively elaborate structure involving several staff members with various specific responsibilities. The author's survey also revealed that experimentation continues and that no one specific pattern has yet been accepted completely.

The fact that team teaching has taken many forms may at first thought disturb the reader. But with further consideration the fact that there is variance in the details of organization and that many different names are used to describe the plans becomes unimportant. The important fact is that the educators realize our traditional teaching methods must be examined and changed in certain situations. The one-teacher control and fixed pupil-teacher ratio concepts of the past are being investigated. Instead of one teacher having more or less complete say over what is taught in his classroom, he is now being asked to plan, teach, and evaluate his instructional program with several other staff members—a team.

Research and experimentation are being carried on which involve both vertical and horizontal team teaching organization. Vertical organization crosses grade lines, whereas, a horizontal organization involves subjects on the same grade level. Although many team teaching programs are horizontal arrangements that take into account students, curriculum, space, and staff on a particular level, there are also many team teaching programs that cross grade lines using vertical organization. A definition that encompasses most of the plans currently included under the term "team teaching" is given in Breve 9.

BREVE 9

Team Teaching Definition

Team teaching is a method of organizing teachers, children, space, and curriculum which *requires* several teachers, *as a group*, to plan, conduct, and evaluate the educational program for *all* of the children assigned to them.

Development of Team Teaching

Team teaching represents further development of two educational trends:

1. *the movement toward more individualization of instruction,* and
2. *efforts to place more knowledgeable teachers before students.*

Efforts to place more knowledgeable teachers in the classroom through organizational planning can be traced from the one-room school to the development of the present-day team teaching programs. (See Breve 10.) Graded and departmentalized school organization plans have enabled teachers to be more knowledgeable but do not seem to fulfill present needs.

BREVE 10

Organizational Continuum Leading to Team Teaching

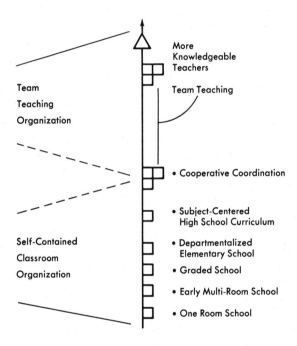

Efforts toward more individualization of instruction have primarily centered upon grouping techniques. By working with a smaller number of students, it was thought that the teacher would be able to better identify and meet the needs of each individual child. In many cases, however, the limiting features of the self-contained classroom curtailed the potential advantages of the grouping arrangements. Today, educators have discovered that the grouping theory combined with the flexibility of a team teaching organization offers promise for greater individualization of instruction.

Team teaching organization is not completely new to education, however. Lancaster and Bell, over one hundred years ago, based an entire system of education on a similar plan. Their teaching team consisted of a professional teacher and selected students utilized as teacher helpers. In 1955 Bay City, Michigan, embarked on a project wherein several classroom teachers shared the services of a teacher aid in a kind of team arrangement. St. Louis, Missouri, did this in 1959, also.

Team teaching as such was proposed in 1956 by Francis Keppel, then Dean of the Harvard Graduate School of Education. In the fall of 1957, it was implemented on an experimental basis in the Franklin School, Lexington, Massachusetts. Dr. John Blackhall Smith, then the superintendent of the Lexington Schools, later introduced the concept into the Dundee School, Greenwich, Connecticut. The Greenwich School has had team teaching in successful operation since 1961.

In 1956 the National Association of Secondary School Principals established the Commission on Curriculum Planning and Development. Later, with the financial assistance of the Ford Foundation's Fund for the Advancement of Education, the NASSP set up a Teacher Utilization Commission to study better approaches to the use of school staff. Of all the ideas developed or gathered by this commission, team teaching seemed to have the greatest potential. J. Lloyd Trump was a key figure in the work of the NASSP Commission at this time. A more detailed account of the early activity in team teaching can be found in the 1958-1967 Bulletins of the National Association of Secondary School Principals.

Of the many institutions of higher education that have been involved in the team teaching movement perhaps the most influential have been Harvard University and Claremont College of California. SUPRAD, meaning School and University Program for Research and Development, is the title used by Harvard University in cooperation with the public school systems of Concord, Lexington, and Newton, Massachusetts. Robert H. Anderson, of Harvard's Graduate School, has been one of the most active participants in SUPRAD. Also aided by the Fund for the Advancement of Education, Claremont Graduate School has been very influential in assisting schools in southern California to develop team teaching programs.

Characteristics

Team teaching as a method of organizing instruction offers the opportunity to incorporate many innovations. Some of them are now generally considered important characteristics of team teaching organization. One of the most important innovations is the use of both professional and nonprofessional personnel with each individual fulfilling specific roles and responsibilities in the operation of the team. The team teaching method also provides for continuous improvement of instruction and of the professional skills of the personnel involved.

Because of its flexibility in grouping students, the team approach can also effectively provide for individualized instruction. The individual is the basic unit of this approach and instruction can be adapted to the individual, or to small, medium, or large sections. Children are grouped and regrouped according to the purposes teachers hope to accomplish with them. Usually, all groupings are considered temporary and are based on the student's ability in a particular curricular area.

The broad and varied utilization of staff along with the flexibility of instructional procedures provides opportunities to further individualize the curriculum. Team teaching allows children to study across grade lines, and especially on the elementary school level where teachers are often "generalists," subject matter specialists are available to work with students. In some situations a single teacher will instruct a group, or individual, whereas, in another grouping arrangement several teachers may be involved. Chapter 3 provides additional information on the various roles that teachers play in a team teaching organization. This flexibility seems to be one of the system's greatest strengths. A summary of the characteristics usually found in team teaching programs is shown in Breve 11.

Many educators seem to use team teaching as a vehicle to bring change to their programs. Since it involves every element of the educative process, it serves this purpose well. The relationships, roles, and duties of the student, teacher, administrator, and other school personnel, the school's facilities, curriculum, as well as the school's salary and other personnel policies can all be affected. In this sense, a move to team teaching organization forces careful evaluation of many facets of the school program and practices.

As stated before, the concept of team teaching has been formed to achieve certain educational goals, such as providing a means of continuous improvement of the instructional program, providing more knowledgeable teachers, and developing greater individualization of instruction. As this concept is applied to the instructional program in different schools, many deviations occur as the local staff, facilities, and interest in the underlying goals vary. Nevertheless, if a school states that team teaching is used, at least the following basic traits should be present:

1. The program should be based on the premise that a good instructional organization will utilize more fully the time and talents of the staff in professional activity.

2. The program must involve two or more faculty members sharing a common teaching effort. If possible, they should provide a spread of specialized abilities.

3. The students should be assigned to the team, not to a specific teacher.

4. The staff, as a team, should cooperatively plan, conduct, and evaluate the educational program. In planning, each teacher has the major responsibility for his particular curriculum interest but receives help from other team members.

Within the framework described here, casual, spur-of-the-moment cooperation and sharing by teachers does not fall within the area of team teaching.

BREVE 11

Characteristics of a Team Teaching Program

■ Cooperative planning, instruction, and evaluation

■ *Extensive* use of audio-visual and other instructional media

■ Flexible scheduling providing time for group planning and study

■ Grouping—flexible arrangements providing for large group, small group, and individualized instruction. Grouping is based on teacher purposes and allows children to work across grade lines.

■ Organization:
   Hierarchy—the team may include a team leader, several specialists, regular teachers, and aides both clerical and technical.
   Cooperative—a group of special or regular cooperating teachers.
   Both organizational patterns call for cooperative coordination of team member activities.

■ Some curriculum alterations

■ Staff—professional (teachers) and nonprofessional (aides)

■ Students assigned to the team, *not* a particular teacher

Organizational Models

In terms of subject matter content, teams can be formed on a "grade" or horizontal basis, "single subject" or vertical basis, or on a "correlated subject" basis. On a grade basis, all of the students assigned to the team are of the same grade level—a sixth grade team, for example. A team organized around a single subject would have only pupils who are studying that particular subject—biology, perhaps. However, in the single subject team, all of the pupils need not be of the same grade level. English and social studies often form the basis for a correlated subject approach to team teaching. Music and art are also favorites of the correlated approach since these two subjects lend themselves to correlation with almost any other subject.

There are two basic models used to organize the instructional staff when forming teaching team units. A "hierarchy" organization is often used. (See Breve 12.) One teacher will be "in charge" of the unit and have several levels of professionals and nonprofessionals working with him. A second somewhat less formal arrangement is also frequently found in which a "cooperative" organization is formed. The cooperative plan is illustrated in Breve 13. Here several teachers plan and carry out the team's instructional program on a cooperative basis with no specific ranks officially designated for the staff members. However,

BREVE 12

Team Teaching Model

Hierarchy

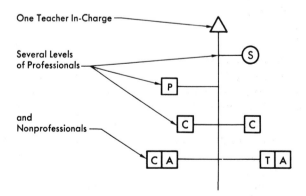

BREVE 13

Team Teaching Model

Cooperative

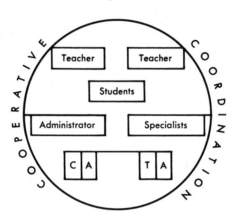

a cooperative unit may elect a team coordinator to assume responsibility for scheduling team meetings, maintaining certain records, facilitating communication, and maintaining contact with the administration.

A third type of team teaching arrangement is the Research and Instruction Unit. However, this represents an adaption of the hierarchy or cooperative arrangement in which a local college or university provides research, evaluation, and instructional consultive aid to the team. One goal of such "R & I" Units is to improve the instructional program through a continuous research and development effort.

Where there are several teams working in a school, an advisory council of the team leaders or coordinators is often formed to work directly with the school's administrator. The purpose of this group is to clarify issues and discuss anything relevant to the effective operation of the teams and school.

One unfortunate effect of "team" teaching is that it seems to suggest teachers who work under other organizational plans do not cooperate or coordinate their efforts. This, of course, is not true. Good teachers have always worked well with their colleagues, sharing ideas, materials, and help, and these same teachers would be excellent staff members of a modern teaching team. The difference lies not with the teachers; it is in the organizational plan. Traditional school organizational patterns make team work very difficult because of their method of assigning students, classroom facilities, time allotments, etc. Team teaching through its method of assigning students, facilities, time, staff, etc., creates opportunities for cooperation, and coordination; indeed there is an obligation to "team up."

Team teaching is not a universal remedy for all that ails our traditional instructional practices. It is a method of organizing teachers, children, space, and the curriculum which emphasizes flexibility and so may provide a teaching-learning climate in which a student can reach his fullest potential. It may be the means of meeting many of the current educational needs of this country, especially the need for greater individualization of instruction and more knowledgeable teachers for the classrooms. However, team teaching is not a finished product and may be just one more step in the evolutionary movement away from the self-contained classroom concept.

3

Team Teaching—Who?

Teacher—A Changing Role

According to most standard dictionaries the term "teach" means "to instruct . . . to give instruction." Traditionally the term "teacher" has referred to the person "in charge" of the instruction. This concept of teacher does not hold true for all situations in a team teaching organization. Team teaching has introduced several new dimensions to teacher behavior and several additional teacher-terms.

In his new role, the team teacher loses much of the autonomy of a single classroom performer. He must work cooperatively with his team co-workers on such tasks as planning a curriculum, assigning instructional duties, and evaluating the instructional program. This new requirement of cooperative effort has important implications for the staffing of team teaching programs. In fact, it has so much importance that only compatible personalities should become members of the same teaching team. Intelligence and technical competence are needed but are not enough to provide the basis for successful team operation. Team teachers must also have a high tolerance for criticism, believe in the group process of decision-making and control, be able to listen as well as express their own thoughts, be willing to concede as well as demand, and be patient, curious, and open-minded. Flexibility may be the greatest overall need of this new breed of teacher.

TEACHER—A CHANGING ROLE

There are a number of terms, some new and some borrowed, which are used to describe a team teaching staff. Generally, these terms fall under two general headings: the professionals and the nonprofessionals.

The Professionals

Team leader, executive teacher, special teacher, senior teacher, master teacher, lead teacher, professional teacher, provisional teacher, regular teacher, and in many cases, the teacher assistant, teacher intern, and cadet teacher are all considered professionals at various levels of preparation. (See Breve 14.) The professional level of a "teacher's" appointment is determined on the basis of special talent, experience, academic background, certification, and degrees earned. All of the professional staff have some teaching responsibility but not necessarily the same authority in the team teaching program.

BREVE 14

Team Teaching Staff
Professionals

Symbols*

■ Cadet teacher   C

■ Executive teacher   △

■ Lead teacher

■ Master teacher

■ Professional teacher   □

■ Provisional teacher   P

■ Regular teacher

■ Senior teacher

■ Special teacher   Ⓢ

■ Teacher assistant

■ Teacher intern

■ Team leader

---

*Symbols used in this text for illustrative purposes.

For certification of team teachers, most states are using the traditional teacher certificates. Therefore, although a teacher may be employed by a particular school district as a "master teacher," he probably will hold a regular teaching certificate. However, certain states, such as Ohio, are reviewing the situation and may begin certifying teachers as "executive teacher," etc., in the near future.

Executive Teacher: Several of the teacher-terms are nearly synonymous. For example, *executive teacher* and *team leader* both refer to the person responsible for the activities of the instructional team. He is "in charge" and is a key figure in all of the planning activities and approves the daily working assignments of the team's staff. He is considered a master teacher and conducts some of the large-group classes. His academic preparation goes beyond the master's degree, and he should have varied classroom experience. Selected executive teacher duties are shown in Breve 15.

BREVE 15

Executive Teacher

Selected Duties

■ Appraises progress of program

■ Coordinates, directs, and schedules team activities

■ Communicates all information to and from the team

■ Makes decisions in certain situations

■ General resource person for the team

■ Encourages and implements research activity

■ Model for his fellow team members

■ Represents the team to administration and community

■ Stimulates thought and action

■ Promotes articulation of team program with other programs throughout the school

■ Orients and assists teachers needing help, especially those new to the team

■ Serves as chairman for meetings

■ Coordinates with the principal, a program dealing with pupil discipline and behavior

■ Keeps abreast of the literature of the profession

■ Serves as a member of the school's Advisory Council

■ Teaches, especially large-group instruction and materials meant to introduce new units

The *executive teacher*, a term which may presently be unique to the state of Ohio, is a professional teacher with team leader responsibilities. In 1966, the Ohio State Superintendent of Public Instruction, Martin Essex, used this term in a Jenning's Scholar Lecture when advancing a new teacher concept. The executive teacher is expected to be an educational leader capable of assessing individual and group needs, planning instructional and curriculum goals, and organizing and directing the efforts of both his fellow teachers and specialists in carrying forward the total program. Since he is an exceptional teacher, the executive teacher should be thoroughly versed in the use of the most modern audio-visual and other instructional media, educational testing procedures, and research.

Many of the duties and responsibilities that are listed here for the executive teacher have been considered supervisory functions in the past. Special area or general supervisors were employed to provide such services, usually on a district-wide basis. Obviously when a school enters a team teaching program and begins using team leaders or executive teachers in the manner described there will be less need for general supervision from outside the local school.

Professional Teacher: The terms *senior teacher, master teacher, lead teacher,* and *professional teacher* refer to a person who has completed a recognized master's level teacher education program, is fully certified by the state, and has had considerable successful classroom teach-

BREVE 16

Professional Teacher

Selected Duties

- Serves as a model for his fellow team members
- Stimulates thought and action
- Gives planning leadership for subject area specialty
- Advises Executive Teacher of special team needs
- Keeps abreast of professional literature in his subject area specialty
- Serves as resource person for subject area with reference to in-service training and curriculum development
- Develops a curriculum resource file for a particular subject area and teaches most large-group classes in that area
- Keeps parents informed through conferences, comments on reports, etc.
- Serves as a teaching member of a team

ing experience. This person should be qualified and expected to teach some of the large-group classes in the area of his preparation and/or interest. This person is also expected to "lead" the other staff members when making academic preparation for classes in the area of his interest. A list of selected duties for the professional teacher is provided in Breve 16.

Provisional Teacher: A staff member who has completed a recognized four-year teacher education program and has state certification but lacks teaching experience is often referred to as a *regular teacher, beginning teacher,* or *provisional teacher.* Some of the duties of such a teacher are shown in Breve 17.

BREVE 17

Provisional Teacher

Selected Duties

■ Shares in cooperative planning of lessons and plans lessons individually for some groups of children

■ Studies cumulative records of all children assigned to the team to determine special needs

■ Keeps parents informed through conferences, comments on reports, etc.

■ Works with fellow team members to improve instructional practices and provide for the needs of the students assigned to the team

■ Teaches most subjects to children in groups of varying sizes who have a variety of needs and who meet in various rooms

■ Directs the work of assigned Cadet Teachers and Aides

■ Serves as a teaching member of a team

Cadet Teacher: Teacher assistant, teacher intern, and *cadet teacher* are terms which refer to the staff member who has not completed a four-year teacher education program, does not qualify for normal teacher certification, but does qualify for minimum or emergency state teacher certification. Usually this person has had little teaching experience. The in-service teacher education opportunities provided by the teaching team organization should be utilized to the fullest extent on behalf of these beginning staff members. Breve 18 indicates some of the services that could be performed by a Cadet Teacher.

BREVE 18

Cadet Teacher

Selected Duties

■ Under supervision, work with pupils in large, medium, and small groups, and individually to:

—Provide appropriate instructional materials
—Explain the purpose of the materials
—Provide meaningful practice to develop mastery
—Provide individual and small group remedial instruction and/or additional instruction to pupils with special needs
—Meet their special needs for information and stimulate their interests and development
—Supervise children when scheduled
—Interpret the school's program to the students

■ Beyond these services the Cadet Teacher will:

—Supervise the work of the Aides
—Design and prepare instructional materials
—Be an active participant in all meetings
—Keep abreast of professional literature
—Assist his fellow staff members with their professional duties.

Special Teacher: The *special teacher* or *specialist* is considered to be in a "staff" position. He is expected to provide special instruction or services in a select area of the curriculum such as art, music, remedial reading, guidance, or physical education. He may or may not be a full-time team member. A functional job definition of one type of special teacher, the music specialist, is shown in Breve 19.

Administrator-Team Relationship

As in a traditional school organization, the principal will be concerned with educational leadership of the total enterprise, general

BREVE 19

Special Teacher

Selected Duties

The Music Specialist

The Music Specialist will act as a full-time teacher of music working under the supervision of the school's principal and the team's executive teacher. He will:

- Provide instruction in music

- Provide the classroom teacher with suggestions for the ongoing program of musical instruction

- Participate in the co-planning of units in which music can enhance deeper learnings

- Be responsible for consultation and execution of culminating activities in which music plays an important part

- Evaluate each child's musical progress for periodic reports to parents

- Advise the principal and executive teacher on the selection and purchase of music supplies

- Keep abreast of professional literature in his field

- Work with the principal and executive teacher in preparing an appropriate time schedule

supervision, administration, and public relations. However, he will find a different relationship developing between himself and the staff. Usually the school's principal deals directly with each teacher, making both long- and short-term teaching assignments, arranging for material support, providing supervisory assistance, etc. In a team arrangement, however, the team leader would assume these duties, in whole or part, for those teachers assigned to his team. The principal would deal with the individual team teacher by working through the team leader. A similar development takes place with regard to the children assigned to the team with the team leader caring for some of the problems that might have traditionally been referred to the school's principal. So, because of the team organization, several different relationships usually form: principal–team leader; principal–staff mem-

INSERVICE EDUCATION POTENTIAL

bers who have some responsibility to the team leader; and principal
—student.

One primary responsibility of a principal working in a team
organization is to coordinate the activities of the several teams. Communication between the teams is essential, and responsibility for this
rests with the school administrator. An advisory council made up of
the several team leaders meeting with the school's administrator and
other specialists, such as the librarian, physical education teacher,
etc., is one technique that is often used to facilitate total school
communication, organization, and administration. Of course, final
responsibility, and therefore final authority, remain with the principal.

He must see that school board policy, system wide rules and regulations, and state laws are fulfilled.

Staff evaluation is one activity that seems to cause some misunderstanding. It should be decided early if the team leader is to share this responsibility with the principal. Ordinarily it is the principal who is expected to evaluate the teachers; however, he may utilize the team leaders in an advisory capacity.

The Nonprofessionals

The employment of nonprofessionals represents an attempt to improve instruction and better utilize highly trained personnel. Most of the proposals for upgrading our educational systems involve the use of some non-certified employees since the use of nonprofessionals seems to be one method of freeing the teacher to teach. In fact, the rising costs of teacher salaries may force school districts to employ substantial numbers of nonprofessionals. The schools of the immediate future will continue to face an economic squeeze, and these financial limitations may require school systems to free the professionals from all non-teaching duties so that they can become planners and instructional leaders. The aims of such a teacher aide program could be stated as:

1. to relieve the professional staff of non-instructional duties,

2. to provide needed supportive services for the professional staff,

3. and to enrich the experiences of children.

In research conducted by the National Educational Association, a clerical aide, technical aide, parent aide, secretarial assistant, paraprofessional or auxiliary personnel, etc., all perform much the same function. All are considered nonprofessionals who relieve the teacher of certain non-teaching duties. This is considered to be the case whether the nonprofessional is paid or volunteers his time. Terms frequently used to describe nonprofessional school employees are shown in Breve 20.

Teachers are often asked to screen the aide applicants but the principal is also involved. The training of teacher aides is usually conducted after the aide is employed by the teacher whom he is to assist. However, teaching adults is a new requirement for most teachers and they sometimes have difficulty working with the aides assigned to them. This situation can be solved to a large extent by a

BREVE 20

Team Teaching Staff

Nonprofessionals

Symbols*

■ Auxiliary personnel

■ Clerical aide   [C | A]

■ Para-professional

■ Parent-aide

■ Secretarial assistant

■ Technical aide   [T | A]

---

*Symbols used in this text for illustrative purposes.

pre-service and in-service training program for both the aides and those teachers using aides. The teacher aide program should begin on a cooperative basis with only those teachers who wish to participate being involved in the initial program. Also, the aide program must have the needs of the teaching team as its focal point.

Recruitment for aides does not seem to be a significant problem. Ordinarily no college education is required but most have completed high school. There is usually an abundance of applicants. The volunteer aide is normally recruited by word of mouth and community organization activity. Many schools offering a paid aide program enlist retired teachers, former substitutes, student teachers, young married women, and persons with community service of some sort.

Clerical Aide: The clerical aide, acting as a secretary to the team, performs those duties usually assigned to a school clerk such as typing, filing, and providing assistance with routine matters of attendance, inventory, and collections, and keeping accurate records of team meetings. Much of a clerical aide's time is spent assisting teachers in preparing materials for instruction and in evaluating students.

Technical Aide: The technical aide's chief functions are to assist in the administration of the school's Instructional Media Center, to maintain audio-visual equipment and other instructional media, and to assist the staff when using this equipment and material. Under certain circumstances he may operate some of the more sophisticated equipment for various teams. Generally speaking, teacher aide duties range from the simple task of listening to providing technical assistance. A list of typical duties assigned to teacher aides is shown in Breve 21.

BREVE 21

Typical Teacher Aide Duties

- Assisting children with their clothing
- Assisting handicapped children
- Assisting on field trips
- Assisting with general classroom routines: distributing supplies, collecting materials, money, etc.
- Assisting with milk program or mid-morning snack, etc.
- Conducting daily health surveys
- Developing bibliographies and doing library research
- Helping with classroom housekeeping
- Maintaining records and inventories and recording other data
- Orienting new students
- Reading aloud and story telling
- Securing, setting up, and operating audio-visual and other instructional media
- Supervising areas outside the classroom such as the lunchroom, playground, study halls, and corridors
- Typing, duplicating, and preparing instructional and evaluational materials and correspondence
- Working with clubs or other student activities

Position Guidelines

The reports of experienced teaching team staffs reveal that there is much to be gained from an early statement of well-defined duties and responsibilities in the form of a job description for each of the categories of professionals and nonprofessionals. This will insure proper job performance and prevent many misunderstandings and conflicts. A special effort should be made to clarify the roles of the school principal, team leaders, and aides. Many problems will be avoided by an early definition of these roles accompanied by a clear statement of the duties and responsibilities of each.

Pre-service training as well as in-service training for all staff members, both professionals and nonprofessionals, is advisable. Consultant assistance in setting up the pre- and in-service programs and the position guidelines is especially important if team teaching is new to the school system. The advice and help of someone thoroughly knowledgeable about team teaching and the development of team organization will do much to insure the initial success of the program.

4

How To Initiate Team Teaching

Developmental Stages

It is important to realize that the term "team teaching" is really an "umbrella" term which covers a large number of instructional arrangements. It refers to a long list of activities starting with the collaboration of two or more teachers dealing with the same group of students and continuing through the "ideal" team teaching situation which is thoroughly planned, fully supplied with staff and the necessary hardware and software, and housed in a school plant designed for team teaching. Breves 22 and 23 illustrate two stages of development along this long line of team teaching activities. The first represents a simple idea or beginning stage of development while the second breve shows a more complex arrangement. In the initial developmental stage the teachers do fulfill the "3 C's" of team teaching, that is, they do communicate, cooperate and collaborate, but each has "his own" students, grading procedures, and classroom. Little compatibility is required in this simple stage since the teachers' involvement with one another is minimal. In the more advanced team teaching stage the students are assigned to the team and not the individual teachers, evaluation and grading procedures are developed by the team for use by all of the staff, and physical facilities are used in terms of the total team's needs. Staff compatibility in this more complex arrangement is imperative for teachers must have a similar outlook on most matters, confidence in each other, be able to plan and work together, and accept both praise and criticism in a professional manner. The average arrangement will fall somewhere between the minimum situation and the team teaching ideal.

No innovation is, of itself, sacred. It is expected that the needs of the local school situation will be honored. However, the essential

BREVE 22

Team Teaching

Developmental Stage
Teacher Responsibility

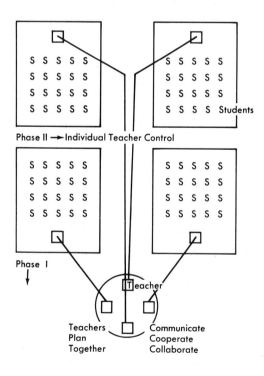

features of the innovation should be kept if it is to be labeled or given the title of the basic idea. But changes of the fringe features of the innovation can be made and this is the right of every group attempting to use the idea. It is the spirit of the innovation that must be respected.

The key to successful entry into a team teaching organization is to

BREVE 23

Team Teaching

Advanced Stage
Teacher Responsibility

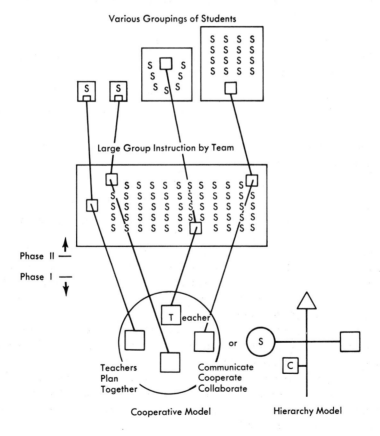

Various Groupings of Students

Large Group Instruction by Team

Phase II

Phase I

T eacher

Teachers
Plan
Together

or

Communicate
Cooperate
Collaborate

S

C

Cooperative Model

Hierarchy Model

realize that the only team teaching organization that will be successful in your school will be one that "fits" the faculty, the physical plant,
and the philosophy of your school system. In other words, your plan
must be "tailor made" for your school.

A Tailor Made Plan

The first step in "tailoring" anything is to measure the situation it
must fit. The philosophy of a school district, faculty attitude toward
experimentation, and community acceptance of change will determine
to some extent the amount of commitment possible. Therefore, before
specific plans are made, those interested in initiating a team teaching
program should:

Examine the school's educational goals as a first step in examining
organizational plans,

make a study of the Team Teaching concept in depth which would
include several visits to schools that have reported using this instructional organization,

determine whether there is any board policy or administrative
ruling that might prevent the immediate initiation of a team approach to instruction,

discuss team teaching with the administrator in charge of the local
attendance unit to be used,

discuss team teaching with the staff members of the school to determine their interest in a team approach to teaching,

and consider community readiness for such an educational change.

If this initial survey reveals that there are no major obstacles to
team teaching, that the administrators are willing to work with the
idea, and that there are several teachers interested in the team plan,
then earnest planning toward the development of a team teaching
organization should begin.

In developing a tailor-made approach to team teaching the planners
should find out the answers to those questions shown in Breve 24.
When this basic, factual information has been compiled, a plan should
be developed that most nearly fits those facts and permits the earliest
possible entry into a team arrangement. Adequate facilities and
money support are likely to follow an enthusiastic, sincere, and
carefully planned beginning.

BREVE 24

Questions Crucial to Planning a Team Teaching Program

- Are there personality characteristics to be considered?
- Can specialists be used? Will their services be available? To what extent will tasks be shared?
- How can time for planning and instruction of staff be scheduled?
- Is a short- or long-term organization most appropriate?
- Should the academic base be a particular area of the curriculum or a grade level?
- Should the team be organized on a hierarchy or cooperative basis?
- What are the teaching specialties or interests of the potential team members?
- Will a team leader be needed? How shall he be selected?
- What clerical assistance will be available?
- What equipment will be available to the team?
- What facilities will be available to the team?
- Does the present school plant lend itself to team teaching?

Community readiness for a team teaching instructional program can play an important part in determining its success or failure. Therefore every available avenue of communication should be used to make known the reasons for the change to this new instructional procedure. The best reason for adopting team teaching is, of course, to improve the quality of instruction. But it must be explained to the parents and other groups just how team teaching will improve the teaching-learning situation. Along with the information presented in Chapter 1 of this text, educators should explain to the public that team teaching can provide for greater community involvement in schools. The use of talented laymen as leaders of student groups can supply new sources of knowledge for school programs, involve local people in improving the quality of schooling, and insure increased community knowledge of the school's program. Team teaching appears to be applicable at every grade level, in any size of school, to any area of the curriculum, for both experienced and beginning teachers, and for students of all ability levels. But if the program is to be successful, careful attention must be given to this area of community understanding and participation in the program.

Initial Operational Plans

The initial team teaching design should be simple, but much thought should be devoted to the determination of educational objectives and procedural guidelines. A plan for the school year or unit to be team taught should be outlined showing general curriculum, teaching objectives, time allotments, and staff assignments by specific activity. Several of the initial planning sessions should be devoted to developing a generally accepted policy regarding such recurring problems as student evaluation and discipline. The school's principal should be present at all such policy planning sessions.

TIME TO PLAN

Not one class should be held until the first specific activities have been planned in detail showing the major objectives, grouping arrangements, space assignments, staff assignments, equipment needed, and an alternate activity in case plans must be altered. This plan and the general plan for the school year should be posted where they will be available to every team member. Planning meetings to develop tentative schedules of teaching activities should be held at least once a week. Adjustment meetings to allow for new developments and take care of problems that arise should be held daily, if necessary.

Although planning periods are often provided for secondary teachers, they are rarely found on the elementary level; however, because group planning is so important in team teaching, great effort should be made to schedule adequate planning time regardless of the grade level involved. Some practices often used to free teachers from instructional duties and provide some planning time include using special teachers (music, physical education, art, etc.) and nonprofessionals, and periodically dismissing certain grades early.

Regular team meetings should also be held which encourage evaluation of the team teaching program and continued curriculum study and development, encourage child study, and discuss teaching techniques. Definite methods for continuous evaluation of the team teaching program should be determined when the initial operating plans are made. Usually such evaluation calls for both objective and subjective appraisal and involves the students, teachers, parents, and school administrator. Specific points which should be considered in the evaluation process are suggested by the following questions:

Are the educational goals of the school and the specific teaching objective of the team being met?

Has there been an increase in the individualization of instruction?

Has the curriculum been improved?

Is there communication, cooperation and collaboration between team members?

Are teacher specialties and interests being used effectively?

Are grouping procedures using large, medium, small and individual arrangements?

Is there good communication between the team, specialists, the administration and parents?

Staff Selection and Development

A point that cannot be overemphasized, and one that is often strongly stated by all who attempt team teaching, is that the members of a teaching team must be professionally compatible. Actually the spirit and attitude of the members will be of more importance to the success of the program than its design. The "I and Mine" must be forgotten in a team arrangement and *involvement* becomes the key factor in success. Team teaching is not an easy task because it attempts to turn theory into practice. A teaching team staff must cooperate, collaborate, and communicate with each other on a very high level of efficiency. Therefore, it is essential that the staff members be mature adults who can deal with one another on a professional basis.

PRE-SERVICE SEMINAR

In many situations teams are formed around available staff. In such a case, the principal can help to insure a good start by seeing that the teams are composed of fairly compatible individuals. Teachers who seem to have different educational philosophies, use very different teaching techniques, or have trouble communicating with each other should not be expected to function well together on the same teaching team. Because of his previous association with them the principal may be best qualified to select those teachers who are most compatible.

Once the members of a teaching team staff have been selected, the development of proper attitudes and adjustment of teaching techniques must not be left to chance. Pre-service training, including orienting and motivating the participants, should begin as soon as possible. Team teaching should not be initiated with an inexperienced team without providing a pre-service program. Also, in-service training activities should be conducted on a regular basis. Much of what is studied during the in-service sessions should be suggested by the team members themselves.

A most fruitful avenue to follow in staff development in a team teaching situation is to utilize the built-in in-service possibilities to the fullest. Faculty and team meetings must be used as the source of much innovative thinking. Also, regularly scheduled team planning sessions which involve a spirit of democratic cooperation must be arranged. These meetings are important since beginning teachers develop and mature quickly when allowed to work with excellent, experienced teachers. In addition, beginning teachers need not accept full responsibility from the first day of their career, for in a team teaching situation it is possible to gradually increase their responsibility under expert guidance. Furthermore, teachers regularly observe each other at work and join in the evaluation of the teaching-learning situation under natural conditions. In fact, team teaching provides the total staff with rare opportunities for professional growth, so long as each team is carefully structured to provide the proper leadership, incentive, and professional examples.

Administrative Adjustments

Since team teaching introduces several new roles to the educational hierarchy some adjustments in the traditional administrative pattern must be made. Most of this adjustment takes place on the local school level. The exact role of the school principal in developing a team teaching organization will depend upon the origin of the impetus for change. The source could be the superintendent, the school's staff, the community, or the principal himself. Obviously his role would vary from one situation to another.

Of all of the administrators involved, the school principal has the greatest adjustment to make with the introduction of a team organization. All of the usual administrative responsibilities of the principalship are present. He is still the educational leader of the school, administrator of the attendance unit, school public relations officer, etc. However, he will deal directly with fewer staff members since teaching teams usually have "leaders," and the staff works through them. This status and the responsibilities and authority of the team leader must be respected by the principal. In most situations the principal will deal with individual teachers through the team leader.

The principal should regularly participate in the planning sessions of all of the teams but should be careful not to dominate them. He should support each team in terms of supplies, space, and time requirements as far as possible. Obviously, he also needs to be as inventive and innovative as possible.

Team leadership is another important point that must be dealt with when forming a teaching team. Not all teams have a designated leader. Some teams prefer to let the leadership role move from person to person as the situation varies. However, it is obvious that things will move along more smoothly if one person will accept the responsibility for certain administrative aspects of running the team. Whether this person is designated as the team leader, secretary, coordinator, or representative, it helps to have one person who will call meetings, arrange for meeting space and other facility requirements of the team, and generally contact people and care for the details of the team's needs.

Appropriate team leadership may begin to emerge during the pre-service training period. The principal should attempt to note this if it should occur, for it sometimes becomes the principals responsibility to designate this person. However, since selection of a team leader can be crucial in the formation of a team, the principal should involve the total team staff in this decision, as far as it is practical.

An advisory council consisting of the leaders of the several teams should be formed and involved in the administration of the school in an advisory role. Although the team sessions and advisory council sessions should decrease the need for total school faculty meetings, they should still be held as needed.

Communication

Communication is going to be of the utmost importance in any enterprise which places considerable importance on communication, cooperation, and collaboration. Thus it is in team teaching. A team member needs to know not only what is expected of him, but what is expected of each individual on the team, the general and specific instructional plans, and the educational objectives for which the team is striving. Such information is not obtained on a casual arrangement. Once again, the importance of group planning sessions in which the entire team participates is brought to light. The most efficient communication will take place when the individual involved is present and participating in the decision-making process at the time the actual decision is made, or when the matter is discussed. For a more detailed discussion of decision-making in a team teaching situation, see Chapter 5.

Written correspondence should not be overlooked in the team's efforts to improve its communication system, however. A form of written communication should be agreed upon by all of the team's staff. It should provide a quick, simple means of communicating when a face to face discussion is not possible. Other definite steps which can be taken to improve communication both within the team and the school are shown in Breve 25.

BREVE 25

Improvement of Communication*

- Distribute the minutes of all advisory council meetings and team leader notices to the entire staff.

- Define broadly, but clearly, the areas in which team leaders serve in an official, intermediary, or other capacity.

- Define and clarify in writing policies regarding such matters as discipline, pupil supervision, etc.

- Allow opportunities for all teachers, above and beyond team lines, to give expression to their ideas and needs.

- Reserve a place for frequently scheduled and productively planned school faculty meetings. Do not allow general school faculty meetings to be superseded by team or advisory council meetings.

*Adapted from *Dundee Team Teaching Project,* A Research Report prepared by the Institute of Field Studies, Teachers College, Columbia University, February 1965, pp. 38-39.

Student Assignment

There are several important points to be dealt with regarding assigning students during the initiating stages of a team teaching program. First of all, how many students should be assigned to a particular team? The answer to this depends, of course, on the number of staff members assigned to the team. A team that has considerable nonprofessional support can deal more effectively with a large group of students than a team with little help of this sort. Generally speaking, however, approximately the same number of children are assigned a teaching team as would normally be assigned to the certified teachers in a traditional system.

As previously stated, the children are assigned to the team as a group, not each child to a certain teacher. In the upper elementary grades and in high school, it is usually considered a means of helping the students develop greater independence. However, it can cause a feeling of detachment, and it may be best to assign younger children to a particular staff person to whom they report each morning. Thus the day can begin in a small-group session with someone the student knows well.

During the initial planning stages of the team teaching organization, the potential staff members should discuss traditional classroom grouping practices as compared to the possibilities offered by a team arrangement. Hopefully the outcome of such a meeting would be an agreement on how students should be grouped with certain guidelines set down in writing. This would provide a basis for an initial grouping of the students assigned to the team. The process by which teaching teams group the students assigned to them is dealt with in detail in Chapter 6. Also, Chapter 11 provides information on methods of assigning students to teaching teams by describing plans that are being used. The reader is referred to these chapters for additional discussion on student assignment.

Curriculum Planning

Primary tasks that habitually confront teachers in a team teaching effort are curriculum formulation and lesson planning. These are tasks common to all teachers in all school settings, regardless of organizational differences, but they assume added significance in a team situation. This is not to imply that in a team teaching situation the authority for curriculum decision-making is transferred to the teaching team, but team teachers, of necessity, have to operate across a more extensive range of curriculum decision-making than do their counterparts in more conventional organizational arrangements.

Team teachers must frequently ask themselves, "What are we trying to accomplish and why?" This question should be raised during one of the first initial planning sessions, and the discussion of it should result in agreement on basic educational objectives that are put in written form for future reference. Because of the social-professional nature of a teaching team, the lesson plan and its objectives must have the approval of the total group. At this point, a strong defense based on sound educational thinking becomes necessary. At this point, the tendency to maintain the status quo for its own sake, hopefully, concedes to logic.

Elements of Successful Team Teaching

Experienced team teaching staffs have found that the ultimate success of a team approach to instruction depends to a large extent on such factors as are shown in Breve 26. In general, any instructional improvement produced by changing to a team teaching organization will depend in large part on the philosophy of the school's faculty, the maturity of the teachers, and the extent to which the student is regarded as the focal point of all planning.

BREVE 26

Elements in Team Teaching Success

- An experimental philosophy in the school district
- Belief that the accomplishments of the team will be greater than the sum accomplishments of the individual instructors
- Keeping the student as the focal point of all planning
- The ability to schedule time for planning and in-service activities
- The leadership available to the team from the administration, the team members themselves, and consultant help
- The maturity and compatibility of the team members
- The support given the team in terms of clerical aide, equipment, and flexible facilities
- Teacher understanding of children and the extent of subject matter preparation

part two

Team
Teaching
Process

5

Decision-Making in Team Teaching

Group Decisions Important

Experience has shown that to be successful, a teaching team must collaborate, communicate, and cooperate. Reports from institutions using the team approach to instruction emphasize that the activities of the team must center around joint planning sessions. Such sessions provide an opportunity for free, open communication and operational decisions which are mutually acceptable to the participating staff. It would seem axiomatic that team teaching staffs should give considerable thought and planning to the decision-making process.

No matter what technique is used to form a teaching team, it will be composed of people of different teaching styles and various types of personalities. If the teaching team is to operate smoothly and efficiently, the people involved must have the use of a thoroughly understood method of arriving at acceptable solutions to the conflicts that are possible. Conflicts will develop as the staff attempts to deal with the problems that normally occur in all learning situations.

Make Good Decisions: Much of the art of making good decisions is in *not* making certain ones. Time should not be wasted on decisions regarding matters that are *not* pertinent, decisions that can*not* be carried out, premature decisions, and decisions for which others have the responsibility. Thus the goals of a good decision-making technique stated in positive terms include: 1) the decisions reached should be pertinent, 2) workable, and 3) appropriate in terms of time and 4) in terms of the authority of the individuals concerned.

The process by which decisions are reached has been analyzed by many, including Mary Parker Follett and Chester I. Barnard. Mary Parker Follett described three strategies by which decisions are reached. She labeled them Domination, Compromise, and Integration.* The terms are fairly self-explanatory. Most would agree that domination and compromise are two strategies used very frequently; however, in a team teaching organization it would be advisable to strive for compromise and integration of possible solutions.

Barnard also suggests three categories for classifying solutions. He describes decisions in terms of their source of stimulus. The stimulus comes from a superior, from a subordinate, or from within the person. Barnard describes this third category as a creative decision. This type, creative decision, is probably the least common in a traditional school organization but becomes very necessary in team teaching.†

Use a System: Almost any situation which involves people, money, position, or physical facilities is likely to require one or more decisions. Team planning continuously centers around these factors. Therefore, many decisions must be made regarding these matters, and it is imperative that definite mechanics be arranged for doing so. If proper procedures are not established, some team members will jump to conclusions under pressure of the moment, and others will be apathetic about many situations.

A systems approach to decision-making is what is needed—a procedure that can be described, understood, and followed by all concerned. Breve 27 shows an approach to decision-making which requires a team to think through its problems and assures everyone concerned an opportunity to contribute to the process. Under these circumstances the decision reached will be far more likely to be accepted and carried through than if no known pattern is followed.

*Griffiths, Daniel E. (Ed.), *Behavioral Science and Educational Administration,* 1964 Yearbook of the National Society for the Study of Education. Chicago, Illinois: The University of Chicago Press, 1964, p. 4.8.

†Barnard, Chester I., *The Functions of the Executive.* Cambridge, Mass: Harvard University Press, 1938, pp. 189-192.

BREVE 27

A Systems Approach to Decision-Making

■ *Identify* true problem (the cause, not a symptom).
Requirement: know the goals involved.

■ *Assemble* known facts and/or additional information.
Requirement: know the research techniques involved—
Computer capabilities
Interaction analysis
Interview
Force field analysis
Questionnaire
Sociometric analysis
etc.

■ *Propose* possible solutions.
Requirement: understand optimal vs. appropriate decisions.

■ *Select* trial solution.
Requirement: understand domination, compromise, and integration of ideas.

■ *Plan* action required to implement trial solution.
Requirement: maximum team involvement.

■ *Act* on trial solution.
Requirement: good communication a "must"!

■ *Evaluate.*
Requirement: know the objectives sought. May require return to third or even first step.

Upon analyzing the decision-making process it becomes clear that there are many factors that must be considered as each problem is examined and each solution selected. Several of the major factors that are commonly involved in most important decisions are shown in Breve 28. Although it may not be necessary to consciously think through each step in the suggested systems approach to decision-making and to consider all of the factors shown, it is well to have such a procedure generally accepted by all concerned for use when the team faces a complex, serious situation.

BREVE 28

Factors That Affect Decisions

■ *Individuals* involved:

> Individuals use and re-use "strategies" in decision-making; that is, they develop "programs" for certain kinds of situations.
>
> Individuals approach decisions with different goals.

■ *Roles* of those individuals involved:

> School board member—administrator—teacher—parent—student—etc.
>
> Initial nature of the "conflict" and the individuals involved puts strong limits on the means available to resolve it.

■ *Groups* involved:

> Formal structure
>
> Informal structure
>
> Many groups want more chance to participate in decisions that affect them, more co-operation, and better quality decisions.

■ *Policies—Regulations—Laws* involved

■ *Philosophies* involved:

> Personal
>
> Professional
>
> Organizational
>
> Official vs. Unofficial
>
> Intended vs. actual

■ *Values* involved:

> Personal
>
> Professional
>
> Groups
>
> Announced vs. actual

Follow-up Important

After a decision has been reached there are still very important steps that must be taken if the action is to have meaning in a team organization. Of primary importance is the communication of the decision to all who need to or want to be informed about it. Here again the importance of good communications is emphasized. Considerable information regarding the importance and methods of improving communications was presented in Chapter 4 and should be reviewed again in connection with follow-up activity for the decision-making process.

At no time is establishing and maintaining of good communications more important than when the staff is involved in decision-making. As far as is practical, everyone concerned with the problem should be involved, allowed to have a voice in the matter, and informed of the decision reached. All of those who are effected by the decision reached must also be informed. Anything short of this may prevent the selected solution from satisfying those concerned with the original problem.

Provisions for implementation of the decision, that is, fulfilling the requirements of the selected solution, are also of utmost importance. The willingness of various individuals and groups to cooperate in implementing the decision will be greatly determined by the opportunity they had to participate in its formation. The benefits that can be derived from following a democratic or group approach become evident at this point.

Evaluation of the entire decision-making process can be a very worthwhile staff activity for it is through this process that a policy, criteria, or procedure for future action can be isolated and called to the attention of the entire staff. The procedure to be followed by a teaching team in arriving at workable decisions should be discussed by the entire staff at an initial planning session.

6

Student Grouping

Grouping Flexibility

Standing high on the list of advantages of a team teaching organization is grouping flexibility. Theoretically speaking, the larger the number of students assigned to a team, the greater its diversity. These two factors, size and diversity, make more flexible grouping possible. However, in practice a reasonable maximum must be recognized when determining team size.

As mentioned before, unless the children are very young, they are usually assigned to a team, not to a particular member of the team. Also, the total number of students assigned to a team should be approximately the same number of students as would traditionally be assigned to the certified teachers on the team's staff. Of course, such rules of thumb should be altered to fit the local circumstances in which a team may be operating. For example, a school system may have an outstanding volunteer aide program in operation that would make possible student assignment on a different basis.

Grouping flexibility is determined in part by the size of the team, and by the number of staff and students assigned to the team. Obviously, the lower the pupil-staff ratio, the greater the opportunity for small-group and individual instruction. A comparison of traditional classroom grouping and the possibilities offered by a team teaching situation should be thought through by each staff member and discussed at a pre-service meeting. Such a comparison is provided by Breves 29 and 30.

BREVE 29

Traditional Grouping Plan*

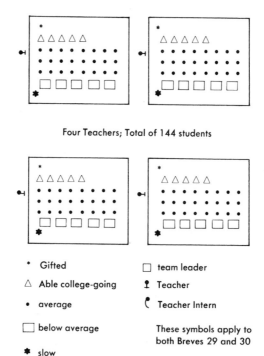

Four Teachers; Total of 144 students

*	Gifted	☐	team leader
△	Able college-going	♟	Teacher
•	average	ℭ	Teacher Intern
☐	below average		These symbols apply to both Breves 29 and 30
✱	slow		

*Reprinted with permission from: "Pupils, Patterns, and Possibilities: A Description of Team Teaching in Pittsburgh," 1961 Annual Report of the Superintendent of Schools, Pittsburgh Board of Public Education, Pittsburgh, Pa., p. 14.

Ordinarily, the larger the total group of students, the more likely that a given team will be able to form subgroups around such factors as ethnic differences and needs, and social differences and needs, as well as the usual factors of intelligence and achievement. On certain

BREVE 30

Team Teaching Grouping Plan*

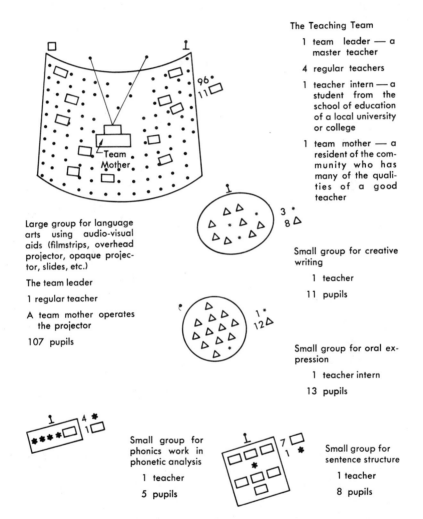

The Teaching Team

1 team leader — a master teacher

4 regular teachers

1 teacher intern — a student from the school of education of a local university or college

1 team mother — a resident of the community who has many of the qualities of a good teacher

Large group for language arts using audio-visual aids (filmstrips, overhead projector, opaque projector, slides, etc.)

The team leader

1 regular teacher

A team mother operates the projector

107 pupils

Small group for creative writing

1 teacher

11 pupils

Small group for oral expression

1 teacher intern

13 pupils

Small group for phonics work in phonetic analysis

1 teacher

5 pupils

Small group for sentence structure

1 teacher

8 pupils

*Reprinted with permission from: "Pupils, Patterns, and Possibilities: A Description of Team Teaching in Pittsburgh," 1961 Annual Report of the Superintendent of Schools, Pittsburgh Board of Public Education, Pittsburgh, Pa., p. 15.

occasions, the teaching staff may wish to separate certain groups for social purposes, and on other occasions, select members for academic purposes. However, as Breve 31 illustrates, team teaching emphasizes the needs of the individual child. The individual's need becomes the basic grouping unit of the team teaching approach. Because of this, all grouping arrangements are considered temporary and subject to change according to the purposes the teachers hope to accomplish with the children.

BREVE 31

Student Assignment

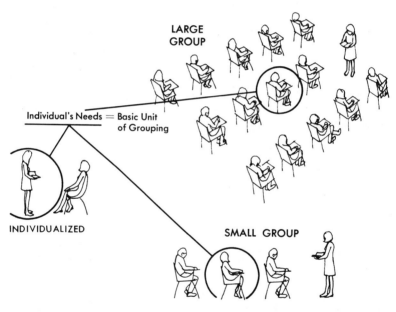

In actual practice, children seem to be assigned to teaching teams on the basis of grade on the elementary level, and on the basis of the subject they wish to study on the secondary level. Scores on standardized achievement tests are important in determining grade placement and so may be thought of as being used in team assignment, also. Certainly where a non-graded arrangement, tracking system, or some other form of ability grouping is being used, test scores, both on achievement and intelligence tests, become very important criteria for team assignment.

The grouping flexibility provided by a team teaching program is of great value in solving problems related to numerical class size, curriculum purposes, teacher competencies, choice of teaching methods, and pupil differences. Guidelines should be developed which take into consideration the various problems that may confront a teaching team yet attempt to keep the individual's needs as the basic unit of the grouping system while permitting grouping according to the purposes the teachers wish to accomplish. Breve 32 is an example of teacher-developed grouping guidelines. Such guidelines should provide for frequent movement of children from group to group as they grow and change. This should be a common occurrence. Most grouping should be on ability level so that a child may be with one group in reading and with an entirely different group in mathematics. However, during some periods all children should be together, perhaps for physical education. In all situations, grouping should be considered temporary.

BREVE 32

Grouping Guidelines

Principles of Appropriateness*

- The size of the group must be appropriate to its purpose.

- The composition of any group must be appropriate to its purpose.

- The time allotments assigned to any group must be appropriate to its purpose.

- The physical and psychological environment must be appropriate to the activities of the group.

- The nature of a task assigned to a team staff member must be appropriate to his talents and interests.

- The nature of the supervision provided for a group depends on the nature and the purpose of the group.

- The subject matter content must be appropriate to each learner in the group.

*Developed by the faculty, Ridgewood High School, Norridge, Illinois.

Large Groups

Large-group instruction would seem most appropriate when:

1. plans call for material that students learn best when explained by others,

2. material to be presented is visual rather than verbal,

3. the major objective is for orientation, motivation, and/or enrichment,

4. considerable technical equipment is essential for reaching the educational objectives,

5. teacher time is an important factor, and

6. children are being taught to listen, take notes, and develop self-control under certain conditions.

The basic purpose of all grouping in a team teaching situation should be to meet a particular need of the students. Fortunately it is possible to care for certain needs of children in large-group arrange-

LARGE-GROUP ACTIVITY

ments. An advantage that is derived from caring for most of the students assigned to a team in a large group is that it frees part of the teaching staff to work with smaller groups of students for remedial or developmental purposes. The fullest advantage must be taken of every opportunity to provide small-group and individualized instruction. Thoughtful team planning is a must in reaching this objective.

Much of the success of a team teaching organization will depend on having appropriate space for large-group instruction. The total number of students assigned to a team probably should not exceed the capacity of the largest teaching facility available to the team on a fairly frequent basis unless closed circuit TV or other arrangements are made to care for a larger group. Physical facilities of present-day school buildings that could be used for large-group instruction are the auditorium, little theater, multi-purpose room, cafeteria, band room, choral room, study hall, school lobby, certain hall arrangements, and kindergarten rooms. Investigation should be made as to the possibility of removing nonbearing partitions in order to create large-group instruction facilities. The basement level of some school buildings can be utilized if remodeled.

Medium to Small Groups

Small groups of students should be formed when:
1. the material to be studied is best learned through student interaction,
2. ideas are to be exchanged and/or discussed, and
3. the goal is to improve personal relations between certain students and groups, or between certain students and staff members.

Possible small-group instruction facilities that could be found in today's school plants are classrooms, library conference rooms, sections of the school cafeteria, storage rooms, certain hall arrangements, and coat rooms in some elementary schools. The remodeling of facilities that are to be converted to instructional uses should be started as soon as possible. Using them before they are remodeled can have an undesirable psychological effect on both students and staff.

Individualized Instruction

At first thought arrangements for individual study might seem to be a small problem. However, because of the need for reference materials

SMALL-GROUP ACTIVITY

and certain other aids, the problem is often the most difficult to solve. The library is a starting point, and classrooms which are equipped with a small classroom library or other reference material will also be of some use. Individual study areas can be erected in many locations in a school building, such as the library, certain classrooms, isolated hall space. Careful thought needs to be given to this problem, and both the teaching team staff and the administration should be as innovative as possible.

An individual instruction situation would seem to be most appropriate when:

1. the material to be covered can best be learned by the student working alone, and

2. the emphasis is on a research or investigating activity.

STUDY CARRELS FOR INDIVIDUALIZED STUDY

Additional information on this topic appears in Chapter 10 where *Individualized and Independent Study* are discussed as an educational innovation.

7

Student Control in Team Teaching

Students involved in team teaching move about more than pupils in traditional school arrangements because they are grouped and re-grouped. Also, they are usually involved in a greater variety of instructional activities and at times may be asked to function more independently. For these and other reasons, student control should be given considerable attention in the administration of a team teaching program. This chapter points out some potential sources of conflict and suggests various techniques which should be considered in planning for adequate student control.

Sources of Conflict

The School's Goals: Certain educational objectives are considered so important to the welfare of this nation that public schools are maintained to guarantee their fulfillment. The curriculum of the public schools usually reflects the dominant values and needs of the current period. Because not all students agree with the goals that are set up for them, conflict may result. The outward manifestation of this conflict usually arises between the student and his teacher; however, the real conflict is often between the individual student and society. He will not agree with or accept the educational objectives established for him. Teachers and administrators must take this factor into account when attempting to deal with disciplinary situations which occur.

Group Influence: Everyone recognizes that groups could not be formed without individuals, but we frequently forget that the individuals who form the group are influenced by the organization they have created. The influence on the individuals comprising the group is a very important factor in student behavior. Whether the organization is a formal one; such as a family, band, or class, or an informal one; such as a gang, club, or neighborhood ball team, it will have an influence on the individual members.

Discipline evaluations usually focus attention on the misbehavior of one child. However, in many situations, the real source of the problem stems from this group influence. Even those behavioral problems which seem to be clearly centered around the behavior of one individual often cannot be solved or handled satisfactorily without a study of the group influences involved. Even if, by careful study of the individual and proper action on the part of the teacher, the source of the child's misbehavior is found and corrected, the problem may not be completely solved in terms of group behavior. The misbehavior of the one youngster has already had its effect on the group and will have a certain aftereffect on both the individual and the class. The teacher will have to be aware of group reactions and influences during the readjustment period.

Also, the teacher must be aware that the student is a member of many groups. He is not only a student but also a member of a class or a team. Teachers should also remember that an individual student may be acting as a member of many diverse groups when none of the groups are actually physically present. To complicate the situation, the influence of any or all of the groups to which the student has allegience can interact, offset, or reinforce one another at any time.

To make matters more difficult, the relationship of one individual to the other members within a particular group often changes. As the group moves from one activity to another the work relationships, authority relationships, social influence relationships and sex relationships change within the group. One individual may belong to several sub-groups within the larger, more permanent group. These sub-groups are formed and re-formed according to the activity of the larger group. No two groups behave precisely the same way although confronted with like situations. Group behavior accepted by one teacher may not be accepted by another, and behavior that is over-looked by the group for one member just won't be tolerated for another. Teaching teams must develop an understanding of group dynamics and a flexible approach to working with groups.

Individual Differences: Different persons look at children's behavior in different ways. A law enforcement officer viewing a young boy or girl is concerned primarily with what the child did or did not do and the evidence regarding the child's activity. A social worker is not so much concerned with what the boy or girl did, but may recognize the behavior as a symptom. A person directly involved in the misbehavior will often be concerned with only the harm that has been done. It is easy to see that much misunderstanding can and does arise because of the various viewpoints of the individuals involved. Teachers need to frequently check their own points of view and reactions to their students' behavior to make sure that it has not become stereotyped.

Before a teacher can cope with abnormal classroom situations, he must have a knowledge of what is considered normal behavior for a particular group of children. He must also be acquainted with those factors that commonly cause children to deviate from normal be-havior. Such knowledge is absolutely essential if a teacher is to deal with the students assigned to his team on a level of mutual respect and cooperation.

No two children are exactly alike, and yet basically, all children are alike. No two children will have exactly the same needs, motivations, or drives at a particular time, and yet all children have basically the same fundamental needs, motivations, and drives. Although a teacher may develop a "rule of thumb" for normal development, he should constantly remind himself that allowances must always be made for individual differences.

It is not difficult to recognize misbehavior; however, it is very diffi-cult to deal with it in terms of the true cause ignoring the symptoms when necessary. We frequently hear teachers state that they simply do not know what to do with a particular student. Often they do not know what to do because they refuse to recognize what the child is saying by his actions. These actions, which may be considered mis-behavior by an adult, may really be a demand for attention on the part of the child. The misbehavior may be the child's mistaken way of trying to belong, to be someone who matters. To bring about a lasting improvement in the behavior of a child, it is imperative that the true cause of his misconduct be recognized and given consideration in the actions that are taken.

One of the keystones of good teaching is the teacher's willingness to seek and understand the reasons behind each child's behavior. It is important to make a special effort to understand those children who need it the most—the noisy ones, the slow ones, the sometimes belligerent ones, those children who are most irritating and unlovable. It is very easy to become indignant and irritated with the offending actions of a misbehaving student. It is difficult to refrain from striking back at the student, his neglectful or lackadaisical parents, and other disinterested people who may be involved. Unlike the sick child, the blind or deaf child, or the polio victim with leg braces, the misbehaving child evokes little sympathy or positive action that promises help. We must remember that it will be treatment rather than punishment that will bring long-lasting results. Of course, it is not only the "difficult" child whom teachers must try to understand but also the "good" child. This child may be bottling up his real feelings. He may need far more help than the outgoing youngster who has been labeled a troublemaker.

Also, at times the underlying cause of persistent discipline problems is the individual teacher. When students talk back to the teacher or attempt to irritate him by other means, such as refusing to follow directions or do any school work, the cause may be the instructor's attitude toward the children and/or his manner of talking to them and dealing with them.

Personal Problems: Poor working conditions such as overcrowded study areas and poor heating or ventilation systems can often be the indirect cause of numerous disciplinary problems. A lack of special programs, equipment, or facilities for the atypical children usually leads to control problems. Children with problems belong in programs that have been especially designed and equipped to help them. When special programs and equipment are not available and the atypical child is held in the regular classrooms, problems occur as a result of his attempts to cope with the situation.

A child's home situation or the negative neighborhood environment in which he lives may contribute heavily to a local school disciplinary situation. The staff of one teaching team can do little to alter these circumstances; nevertheless, they must be aware of them, allow for their influence, and compensate for them whenever possible.

A child who is hungry or tired is very apt to become a discipline problem. A teacher should periodically analyze each group as to proper rest and diet. Also, being aware of certain physical and mental defects can help a teacher avoid many difficult classroom situations. The school's cumulative records can greatly assist the team in learning about each child.

Techniques for Control

In more cases than not, the initial impulse of a teacher when responding to a disciplinary situation is one of anger, resentment, and often, personal hurt. This reaction only defeats the teacher's efforts to maintain a good learning situation. In cases where there is an attempt on the part of the child to hurt the teacher, the situation is only worsened by responding with a personal reaction.

All teachers have discipline problems. Some teachers have many and others have relatively few. But teachers do have them and some are of such a persistent nature that the teacher may feel he is sure to lose his temper or do something desperate. Techniques to safeguard these situations are needed. Every team should recognize the possibility of such a situation developing and have a plan of action that will safeguard the instructors by giving temporary, immediate relief to the situation. This will give the student time to think and cool down. It will also provide for the intervention of another staff member if the situation seems to merit this. Theoretically team teaching provides a reprieve for both student and teacher in case of conflict, but still fewer critical situations will occur if the team has planned to utilize certain techniques.

Preventive Techniques: Good teachers realize that our modern discipline, with its emphasis on self-control and self-direction, is one of the most difficult things a child must master in our rapidly changing, complex social framework. They realize that any contribution they may make toward helping their students develop good citizenship and self-control will depend upon their skill in managing the pupils in a manner which conforms to a psychology of self-direction.

An understanding of the students' background, religion, home, and neighborhood is essential to maintaining good discipline. But in good disciplinary situations the whole often seems to be more than the sum of the parts. If a team is maintaining an adequate teaching-learning situation, the members will:

1. provide a situation that is free from serious distractions,

2. develop and support respect for authority in the classroom and in the school,

3. develop student ideas, interests, and skills which contribute to self-control and good citizenship, and

4. attempt to present a dynamic but child centered teaching-learning atmosphere.

To consistently maintain a good climate for learning, the staff's attitude toward the children must be a positive one. An attempt to understand the child's side of each situation and to understand the factors that might be affecting his behavior is necessary. In general, each teacher must try to comprehend children—their youth, vigor, joy, and potential,—yet remember that they are insecure, full of doubt, and wanting to please. The good team will encourage, stimulate, and invite children to behave, participate, and learn. Other characteristics that are important in maintaining a good teaching-learning situation are a flexible attitude, a responsive nature, and the ability to be straightforward when necessary.

The establishment of mutually meaningful standards is the very foundation of good discipline. Therefore, the team should, very early in the school term, discuss with the students what standards should be accepted by the group. This prevents many problems which might result from ignorance of what is acceptable, carelessness, or an attempt to see how far one can go. To do this effectively, however, each teacher must:

1. be free from any driving need to be liked by all of the students,

2. accept the role of the "parent figure,"

3. realize that boys and girls don't want to be given absolute freedom to do whatever they please, and

4. be consistent in upholding the adopted standards.

Specific routines should be taught to help the students take care of the many reoccurring classroom situations in which they are involved each day. Also, the staff must accept their part in these routines and play the part with persistence. Routines dealing with the distribution of books and paper, making assignments or giving directions, student seating, and the forgotten pencil must be worked out. In fact, all of the small details that occur and reoccur must be given careful consideration by the teaching team and definite plans must be made regarding them.

Often teams use student monitors to expedite various established routines. This is an educationally sound practice but should not be done hastily since the efficiency of the monitor program depends on the selection of reasonably reliable students. Also, the monitor's function and duties should be carefully defined.

Keeping a class busy is another practice that has much to recommend it in terms of maintaining satisfactory student control. A five- or ten-minute assignment written on the board each morning will encourage the class to come into the room promptly and settle down to their schoolwork. This policy of keeping students busy with interesting, well-planned assignments applies not only to the beginning of the school day but to the last few minutes as well.

Teachers sometimes talk too loud, or on too high a pitch, or often, simply too much. Good teachers learn to listen to themselves, stop talking, and then continue again in a tone that is free from anger, annoyance, or anxiety. Children resent being yelled at, much less screamed at, and will often react in a hostile manner. Many very successful teachers have used such signals as the lights, a small bell, or putting a finger to the mouth to silently request that everyone lower their voices.

As teachers we need to constantly remind ourselves that the attention span of children is very short. If children are held on a particular activity too long, general restlessness and noisiness seem to grow spontaneously. This should be considered when lesson plans are made, of course, but when it happens during the school day, the work under way should be changed before the noise gets the upper hand.

Since many discipline problems arise out of situations in which a student or a few students cannot do the assigned task, it would be well for the teaching team to individualize instruction wherever and whenever possible. It is better to have a modified version of the general assignment completed by the less capable student than to have the same boy or girl become a disciplinary problem.

Professional teachers realize that one of the best ways to improve their teaching effectiveness and, also, to avoid disciplinary pitfalls is to welcome classroom visitation by fellow professionals. Supervision encourages the teacher to work for the best possible classroom control. Supervisors may notice that antagonistic or belligerent pupil attitudes are caused by certain teaching techniques. They may also notice an instructor's flippant or sarcastic remarks or unfriendly looks of which he is completely unaware. He then can take corrective action before the situation reaches the problem stage. Team teaching, of course, provides many opportunities for one professional to observe another.

Sincere, polite, constructive criticism should be the rule, not the exception.

Corrective Techniques: Teams must learn to plan preventively in regard to disciplinary problems. However, not all disciplinary situations can be avoided or controlled by preventive techniques. Situations sometimes develop too rapidly or unexpectedly. The team should recognize the possibility of such a happening and should think through various techniques that can be followed.

Opinions differ as to when a classroom situation should be considered serious. Most agree, however, that in terms of the trouble it can cause, there are several stages in the development of a serious disciplinary situation. These stages usually involve: whispering and inactivity; laughing, talking, writing notes, and horse-play; then the

BREVE 33

Professional Teacher Behavior

■ Accept and appreciate each student as a human being and always attempt to maintain a positive and instructive attitude toward all students.

■ Be reasonable, patient and consistent.

■ Choose words carefully. Remember that a teacher's special choice of words will be an important factor in motivating a response from the children involved.

■ Learn to recognize "overloaded" or "symbolic" issues and to keep them in proper perspective.

■ Look at the whole situation diagnostically and do some thinking about the future. Look at the facts in their "situational context."

■ Never react to classroom misbehavior personally but preserve an objective point of view.

■ Try to become sensitized to the proper "timing" for handling disciplinary situations.

■ Try to express approval in a time, manner, and place that is acceptable to the students concerned.

■ Try to locate the cause, not the symptom, of the trouble.

completely disorderly state, which often includes tripping and punching, throwing missiles, calling names and showing obvious disrespect for the teacher. Certainly a situation that involves either of the last two stages should be considered serious.

In his efforts to correct the situation, the teacher should keep in mind that the seriousness of the problems he will face tomorrow may be lessened by the way he acts today. If he teaches in a professional manner, he will behave as suggested in Breve 33.

A fruitful step to try when confronted with a serious disciplinary situation is to contact the child's home. Often a short note to his parents, a brief phone call, or, if necessary, a short visit to the home will bring the family and school into close cooperation in attempting to solve the problem. It is important for a teaching team to be acquainted with the various services provided by the school system which can be used in attacking serious classroom situations. Over and beyond this, the staff should be familiar with the various agencies and individuals in the community as a whole who can be called upon to deal with very serious or unusual problems.

There are times when a pupil should be sent from the classroom. A good practice is to say just a few words to the child at the door to let him know why he is being sent out. Sending an offending pupil from the group is one of the most frequently used methods of classroom control; however, to insure that the practice is not overworked, a teacher should send a child from the group only when the best interest of the class demands it. Also, before sending a child from the group, the teacher should consider using various alternate disciplinary approaches.

Leadership: The importance of the staff's attitudes and behavior in setting a good example for the students cannot be overemphasized. Children behave so much like the adults around them that it is at times almost comical. Of course, it is flattering for the teacher to have a student imitate him, but it also illustrates the tremendous influence the teacher has upon the child. Anything we do before children, for good or ill, remains with them longer than we can imagine.

Perhaps no teacher can be a prestige image for every one of his students, but he may have certain capabilities in the science laboratory, in the gymnasium, in the shop, or on the playing field which will enable him to provide a good example for many of them. Certainly each teacher should strive to be an honest, authentic, genuine, unique person and thereby encourage his students to do the same. Schools need to make the most of their natural prestige figures.

Studies to determine the personal qualities of successful teachers tend to give the impression that a good teacher is a "Super-Person" with godlike qualities. We all know, however, that teachers are just plain people. Still, successful professional teachers are distinguished by both the qualities they possess and the degree to which they possess them. Breve 34 presents a selected list of such qualities.

BREVE 34

Professional Teacher Characteristics

Selected-Personal Qualities

- Does not use his students to work out his own problems
- Has at least average intelligence but knows his own limitations and works within that framework
- Enjoys good physical, mental, and emotional health
- Is willing to serve others with a sense of humility and modesty
- Stands up for what he believes to be worthwhile; is a person of integrity and good judgment
- Expresses ideas clearly in speech and writing
- Organizes and delegates responsibility
- Obtains the cooperation of others
- Has definite life purposes and objectives
- Faces reality with imagination and self-confidence
- Has a good sense of humor
- Is enthusiastic and energetic

There is no one characteristic or group of characteristics that guarantee successful leadership. No single quality will enable an observer to select a particular teacher as a leader. No hereditary or environmental background assures that a person will have leadership qualities. Leaders conform to no single pattern. Most educators would concur in the belief that teacher leadership can be acquired, but few people develop leadership qualities overnight. In teaching, the leadership relationship is built over a period of time as the teacher and class work together. A teacher can do much through his leadership to help establish a favorable school atmosphere and thus help to prevent undesirable behavior.

Most teachers plan carefully for the teaching-learning situation. Yet, they generally conduct a hit-or-miss program in planning for possible disciplinary situations. It is better to be a leader than to be lead by developing predicaments. In attempting to maintain satisfactory student control, there is no substitute for forethought.

Seeking Assistance: Most believe that the first staff person involved in a disciplinary situation should attempt to settle it. If the situation is a difficult one, or if additional help is wanted, perhaps the next person involved should be the staff member to whom the child reports first each morning. With small children this staff member may act as a "homeroom" person and may have more influence upon the child. The exact role of the team leader in disciplinary situations must be decided on an individual team basis. Individual personalities and capabilities must be taken into consideration in making this decision. In very serious situations the problem should be called to the attention of the school's administration.

From time to time a team will encounter a child who is beyond their capability to help. They must know when to request outside help. The student may need more extended treatment or therapy than the staff is capable of rendering. The team and special school personnel must know what resources exist locally and even on the state level. Knowing how and when to use these resources in the study-diagnosis-treatment process is imperative.

8

Team Teaching Hardware and Software

A Multi-media Activity

Children grow and learn in many ways—intellectually, socially, emotionally, and physically. Team teaching provides for the most efficient growth of each child through experiences that are varied as well as broad. Team teaching presents each child with a variety of educational experiences and class organizations as he seeks to achieve some measure of independence and strives to learn at his own pace. An important technique used to provide such a broad and varied educational program is the extensive use of modern teaching hardware and software. The extensive use of this modern instructional equipment or hardware and the teaching materials or software designed to accompany it has become a hallmark of team teaching, as it is of good teaching in general. Good teaching teams make extensive use of audio-visual and other types of instructional media, thus providing variety in the teaching procedure.

Current literature uses several terms to describe the facilities and equipment which support the teacher in his instructional efforts. The term *audio-visual* has never been thought to be completely satisfactory, since it is not considered to include books and other library materials. The term, *Library-Materials Center,* includes books but this still seems to be limited. The impact of educational technology on teaching methods has created a need for a more encompassing term which would include everything a teacher might use in his efforts to help students learn. *Educational Materials Center* is being used by some as well as *Instructional Resource Center.* However, the term *media* appears in some federal legislation which provides financial support in this area; thus, the title *Instructional Media Center* is used throughout this text. However, regardless of what title is used, the purpose of such a facility is to provide equipment, materials, service, as well as both pre-service and in-service training to assist the staff in its instructional program.

The Instructional Media Center

The development of educational technology, especially within recent years, has greatly increased the amount of material available for equipping the modern school. Educational technology is producing both relatively simple devices and complex systems such as the computer assisted programs for individualizing instruction. Most educators recognize the important role of the new instructional media and also the fact that much remains to be done in linking this new media to the attainment of our goals. It is quite apparent that a team teaching program will be completely functional only when provisions for the effective use of educational technology have been completed. For example, the Instructional Media Center (IMC) must contain equipment and facilities to support large- and small-group, independent, and individualized instruction as well as more traditional instruction, since the team teaching concept demands maximum flexibility and usability of instructional equipment.

Every teacher has available to him an abundance of illustrative material: photographs, tearsheets, books, magazines, and solid objects. Materials for many interesting and informative presentations are free and easily acquired. For example, clippings from periodicals often form the basis for group discussions in history, geography, and current events. The difficulty usually is finding the best way to present them to the group. A whole class cannot intimately view small objects from their seats, and every teacher knows the disadvantages and disturbances that are invited by passing materials around the room. Yet, the lesson would be vastly improved if each student could see clearly what was being shown. At this point the IMC can perform a most valuable service, both to teachers and to their students. With the help of the facilities and equipment of the IMC, full utilization of these sources of material can be a reality. By the use of the opaque projector a clear picture can be projected on a screen of any magazine illustration, page from a book, solid object, etc. which the teacher may wish to use. Transparencies to be used on the overhead projector are easily made from magazine illustrations, other materials, or from the teacher's own suggestions.

The Instructional Media Center should provide for the most efficient use of audio-visual hardware and software. Such centers include (1) a working and training area for the preparation of materials, (2) a graphics section for the production of specific curriculum needs, (3) a recording facility used to add auditory cues to visual materials produced in the graphics section, (4) a materials distribution section, (5) an equipment maintenance section, and (6) an administrative section for necessary direction and record keeping.*

Exactly what the IMC should contain is, of course, up to the individual school system. The goal should be a rather comprehensive center using the school library as a hub and providing for storage, maintenance, in-service training, and administration of all audio-visual hardware and software, as well as providing a work area for the preparation of teacher-made material, both audio and visual.

The IMC should be more than just a storage area or preparation area. It should be a dynamic, innovative place where new thinking is encouraged and technical skills are utilized to incorporate new ideas. Such a center not only functions as an aid to faculty presentation, but also allows students to become acquainted with the learning center concept. As new materials are developed, the IMC should provide teachers with an understanding of how they apply to the problems of teaching and learning. Some of the activities that could be carried on in the IMC are indicated in Breve 35.

Equipment and Materials

In team teaching the prime question that is raised repeatedly is, "What should we be doing, or planning to do, in order to improve our teaching?" A concomitant question is, "What kind of equipment is needed to teach most efficiently and effectively?"

---

*Dan Echols, "The Making of a Media Center," *Audio-visual Instruction,* XII, October, 1967, p. 799.

BREVE 35

Instructional Media Center Activities
Selected List

■ Evaluation of program, services, and equipment

■ Independent study or individualized instruction

■ Pre-service and in-service staff training

■ Production of teacher designed instructional materials

■ Requisition of materials, service, and equipment as needed

■ Acquisition of reference and resource material for students and staff

■ Storage, maintenance, repair, distribution, and administration of instructional media

In terms of equipment, a comprehensive instructional center should include chalkboard, display board, flannel board, demonstration materials for illustrating basic concepts in mathematics, science, etc., the school's materials for programed instruction, simulation, and gaming experiences, the school's computer-assisted instruction equipment (CAI), and related materials. All of the traditional audio-visual equipment would be housed in the IMC, also. Breves 36 and 37 show a suggested list of hardware and software that could be included in a comprehensive Instructional Materials Center.

Proper use of the IMC hardware and software is timesaving in teaching because it makes it possible to present a wide variety and amount of material in a short time, building a common background for the whole group; it is possible to present many things in detail that would otherwise be difficult, and learning can take place at a faster rate than would otherwise be possible because the variety and pace motivate the students and maintain their interest. Also, the IMC helps the teacher by presenting material and instruction in certain specialized areas, thus providing experience not easily obtained any other way.

The motion picture is almost a traditional example of how IMC material and equipment can assist the teacher in presenting a lesson. When films are used, the world's leading experts can be brought into the classroom. They concentrate on their areas of specialization and

BREVE 36

Instructional Media Center Hardware
Selected Items

■ Chalkboards—portable

■ Computer-assisted instruction equipment

■ Demonstration centers—portable, for mathematics, science, etc.

■ Display boards—portable

■ Duplicating and copying equipment

■ Flannel boards (felt boards)—portable

■ Microfilm and microfiche readers

■ Previewer equipment, film, filmstrip, slide

■ Production equipment for both auditory and visual (graphics) instructional materials

■ Projection screens—portable, rear projection

■ Projectors—film, filmstrip, opaque, overhead, slide

■ Public address system—portable

■ Radio

■ Reading equipment—remedial, speed, etc.

■ Record players

■ Stereographs

■ Tachistoscope

■ Tape accessories (splicers, storage equipment)

■ Tape recorders

■ Television and kinescope

provide an accurate presentation. Accuracy is an important quality of almost all IMC materials.

The use of IMC hardware and software increases the teacher's effectiveness; however, these devices are constructive teaching aids, not substitutes for good teaching. Accurate and interesting, they can stimulate thinking and an awareness of basic concepts. At all levels,

BREVE 37

Instructional Media Center Software
Selected Items

- Cartoons, charts, drawings, pictures, posters, study prints, etc.
- Computer-assisted instruction materials
- Films
- Filmstrips
- Gaming activity materials
- Globes
- Instructional tapes
- Maps
- Microfilm and microfiche instructional materials
- Prepared exhibits on various subjects
- Records
- Reference and general library materials related and coordinated to the total IMC
- Resource file for approved field trips
- Simulation activity materials
- Slides
- Transparencies

using the IMC permits competent teachers to provide increased learning opportunities and still preserve the personal relationship between teacher and student. IMC materials can capture the imagination of young students. For example, boys and girls can see how people live in Africa, in the rain forests of the Amazon, in the snow-capped mountains of Switzerland, and even behind the Iron Curtain. They can explore the United States from coast to coast. Through the use of such materials students not only gain factual knowledge and understanding of other places and people but also develop better attitudes toward school.

An example of a newly developed teaching tool that is found in some progressive IMC's is CAI, Computer Assisted Instruction. Originally, the computer was used to simulate teaching machines, but later it was discovered that it could contribute to the teaching process. Computers should have a dramatic effect on education since they can help students solve problems and locate up-to-date information. Computer-based teaching devices, programed and operated by trained teachers, may be the basic instructional tool in the IMC of the future. Chapter 10 provides a more detailed explanation of computer assisted teaching.

Federal Funds

Numerous sources of federal aid are available to schools for purchasing modern instructional materials. The National Defense Education Act for example, provides for the use of educational films to help strengthen instruction in science and mathematics. Each state is entitled to acquire instructional films and other audio-visual materials, whereby local, county, and city school systems may match funds with those furnished under the act.

The school superintendent, curriculum director, IMC or audio-visual director, or coordinator of federal projects should be consulted for correct local information. He will be acquainted with the plan for his state and can help determine the procedure to be followed in making a request for materials. The assistance of the Instructional Media Center coordinator should be sought whenever plans for the IMC are being made.

Instructional Media Center Facilities

The Instructional Media Center should serve not only as a depository for books and other learning materials but also as the location of curriculum and instructional material for the professional staff. It should serve as the center for student research and independent study, too. Information should be easily attainable from many sources. Seminar rooms should be provided where the student or teacher can review and/or discuss movies, filmstrips, tapes, etc. Seating arrangements should include individual study carrels, small work area spaces, and informal, comfortable furnishings for reading and study.

The center should be planned with a view toward openness and easy access from all parts of the building. Versatility would appear to be the key word. Careful planning is a must when establishing an IMC, for it will be the very "hub" of a modern team teaching organization.

Instructional Media Center Staff

It is obvious that the person assigned the responsibility of administering an IMC must be a highly trained professional. We here must make a clear distinction between the nonprofessional technical aides assigned to teams who *assist* with equipment and materials and the

BREVE 38

Duties of an Instructional Media Center Director*

- Administers the Instructional Media Center, its services, and programs
- Evaluates the IMC and its programs
- Evaluates materials, equipment, and personnel in relation to the total IMC
- Helps in organizing procedures for selecting and purchasing IMC hardware and software
- Interprets the IMC program to administrators, teachers, supervisors, and the public
- Informs teachers of the conditions of use of available hardware and software
- Provides help and guidance for teams on problems related to materials
- Provides pre-service and in-service staff training
- Produces specialized materials and programs for teachers when needed
- Works with total staff to improve the quality of the IMC
- Works with total staff in developing long-range plans for IMC

---

*Adapted from Edgar Dale, *Audio-visual Methods in Teaching,* Revised Edition (New York, N.Y.: The Dryden Press, Inc., 1954), p. 519.

professional who *is in charge* of the IMC, often designated as "coordinator" or "director." This professional must not only know the IMC hardware and software but understand the teaching-learning situation thoroughly. A look at Breve 38 will show possible duties of an IMC director and will emphasize the need for a professional educator to serve in this highly technical position.

9

Team Teaching School Facilities

Desirable Features

Obviously, any plan that affects the pupil-teacher ratio and the curriculum as team teaching does is very much dependent on the physical facilities available. There is little sense in planning for large-group instruction if there is no facility capable of accommodating a large group of students. In fact, some educators believe that it is best to postpone entry into a team teaching program until adequate facilities are available; such is the importance of facilities in a team teaching situation.

The characteristics of a team teaching program, as illustrated in Breve 11, suggest that an adequate team teaching facility should be capable of accommodating groups of various sizes, facilitating change from one grouping arrangement to another, providing easy access to the Instructional Media Center, and providing space where each staff member or the total team can prepare plans and materials. This latter area could be considered a "center" for team activities. Also, each student should have a place which he can consider "his." This place should provide storage for his belongings and, if possible, a

STUDENT STORAGE AREA

study area. Such an arrangement can also be utilized by each student for individualized or independent study under certain circumstances. Other features that would be desirable in a team teaching situation are shown in Breve 39. A desirable arrangement of such facilities is illustrated in Breve 40.

To Build or to Remodel

No one would deny that it is certainly wonderful, and perhaps psychologically stimulating to have a new physical plant in which to operate; however, few would say that a team teaching program requires a new building of special design. As stated above, team teaching requires a certain flexibility in physical facilities, but whether this is achieved by innovative remodeling or building a new structure is not really important. There are many successful team teaching programs being conducted in remodeled school buildings.

BREVE 39

Desirable Features of a Team Teaching Facility

■ Centrally located and easily accessible Instructional Media Center

■ Multi-use areas, i.e. multi-purpose rooms, little theatres, etc. that can be utilized in many ways

■ Space accommodations for groups of various sizes including large, medium and small groups and individual study. Classrooms of various sizes and movable partitions are recommended

■ Space for teachers to meet, plan, and work together

■ Sufficient flexibility in space arrangement to permit rapid shifting of group size and moving of students into new grouping arrangements

Probably the total number of students assigned to a team should not exceed the capacity of the large-group instructional facility available to the team unless other arrangements, such as TV instruction, are also available. Much of the flexibility of team teaching revolves around

FOLDING SOUNDPROOF WALLS

BREVE 40

Team Teaching Facilities Relationships

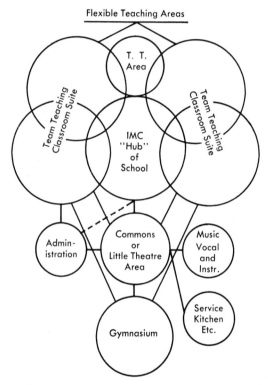

Flexible Teaching Areas

T. T. Area

Team Teaching Classroom Suite

Team Teaching Classroom Suite

IMC "Hub" of School

Admin- istration

Commons or Little Theatre Area

Music Vocal and Instr.

Service Kitchen Etc.

Gymnasium

the ability to utilize large-group instruction. Therefore, facilities and equipment for a large group are a must.

Auditoriums, school theaters, multi-purpose rooms, cafeterias, band rooms, choral rooms, study halls, school lobbies, some hall arrangements, kindergartens, etc. are representative of present-day school facilities which, with proper remodeling, can be utilized for large-group instruction. The replacement of nonbearing walls by movable partitions has been successfully used to create large-group instructional areas from two or more traditional classrooms in many school buildings.

In new structures that have team teaching in mind when they are designed, classroom suites which are the equivalent of two, three, or more traditional classrooms are often connected in an "L," "H," or "4 square" arrangement. Breve 41 shows the floor plan of the Sylvania Whiteford Elementary School which uses the "L" shaped instructional area. An example of the "H" design is provided by Findlay Elementary School shown in Breve 42 while Breve 43 shows a "4 square" design that was recommended for the Crestline Middle School. Accoustically treated movable walls and movable furniture are used to create smaller grouping arrangements. A centrally located little theatre or "commons area" is also used to provide large-group facilities. The Instructional Media Center is usually at the "hub" or center of such arrangements.

Medium- and small-group facilities are often developed from existing classrooms, library conference rooms, small sections of the school cafeteria, storage rooms, some hall arrangements, and coat rooms. Modern buildings provide for smaller groups by using movable furniture, such as storage units and bookcases on rollers, the movable wall, and providing a variety of classroom sizes.

Many locations in present day school buildings can be used for the erection of individual study carrels. The outer walls of the library, traditional classrooms, and isolated hall space, etc. provide possible locations. Plans for any modern schools buildings should provide special areas for individual and independent study.

Flexibility in utilizing space is one of the primary objectives of modern school design, but it can often be achieved in remodeling older structures if careful thought is given to the problem. Care must be exercised even if a new building is in the offing, however, for a new structure will not guarantee flexibility. In terms of modern space utilization, many so-called "new" school buildings are outdated the day the doors open. An indication of the kind and amount of space flexibility needed in a team teaching situation is provided by the Dundee School, Breve 44. The architects studied the concept of team teaching and translated the needs into a physical plant which would provide the flexibility needed for this new pattern of school organization. New construction specifically designed for a team teaching program should have many of the features previously suggested in Breve 39.

Adequate Equipment

In addition to "space," team teaching requires adequate equipment. Large-group instructional areas should be equipped with the necessary instructional media, such as overhead projectors, blackout curtains, etc., so that the teacher's emphasis can be on a first rate presentation rather than on securing the equipment needed to conduct a large

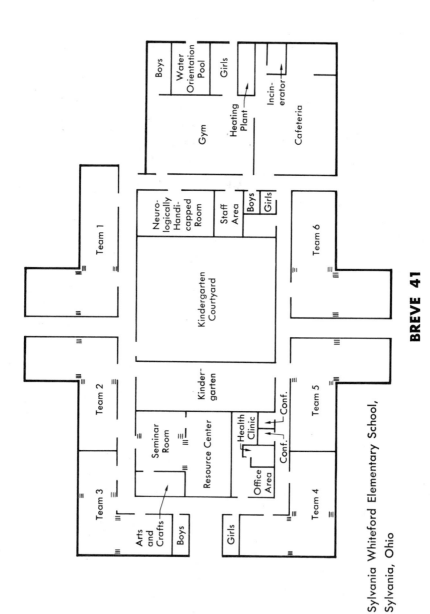

BREVE 41

"L" Instructional Area

Sylvania Whiteford Elementary School,
Sylvania, Ohio

98

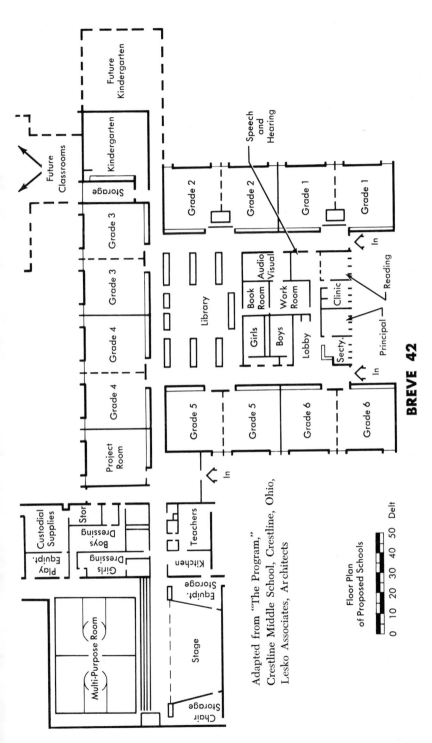

BREVE 42

"H" Instructional Area
Elementary School, Findlay Public School District

Adapted from "The Program,"
Crestline Middle School, Crestline, Ohio,
Lesko Associates, Architects

Floor Plan
of Proposed Schools

0 10 20 30 40 50 Delt

99

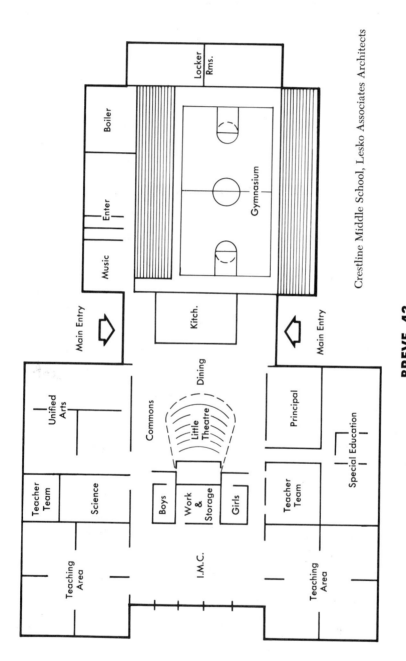

Crestline Middle School, Lesko Associates Architects

BREVE 43

"4 Square" Instructional Area

Dundee School

The Perkins and Will Partnership, Architects, Chicago, Illinois.

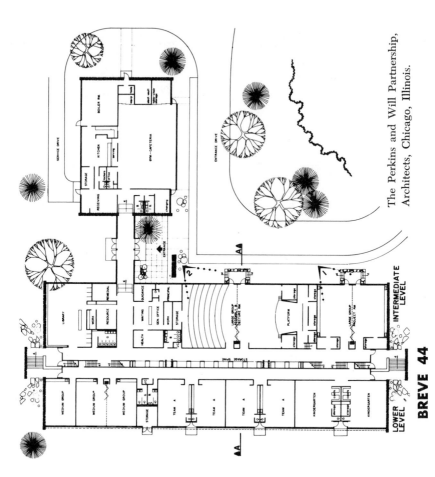

The Perkins and Will Partnership,
Architects, Chicago, Illinois.

BREVE 44

Dundee School

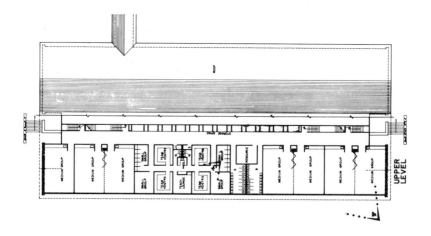

class. The Sylvania Whiteford Elementary School has combined the audio-visual equipment commonly used in most classrooms into a movable "communications wall" which is located in each large-group team teaching area. Independent study, discussion, or seminar rooms as well as large-group lecture rooms must be appropriately equipped with overhead projectors, public address systems, and comfortable seating. And the list of necessities keeps growing because successful team teaching schools find they need more equipment rather than less as they improve their use of team methods.

Arrangements for individualized and independent study are often complicated more by the need to have special materials and equipment located in the study area than by space requirements. Providing general reference materials and special equipment and materials for any number of study carrels is a problem. However, a start can usually be arranged through the innovative use of school library materials, the redistribution of classroom library materials, and careful purchase of a limited quantity of additional materials.

Sources for Building Ideas

In the area of school plant planning, new and innovative ideas are brought forth every day, and it is best to seek advice on current thinking at the time of construction or remodeling. The School Facilities Council and the American Institute of Architects are excellent sources of information. Professional periodicals are also a source of descriptions and models of recently designed team teaching school facilities. The federally funded Regional Educational Laboratories or Centers will provide current information on school plant planning. Chapter 11 of this text describes various team teaching patterns that have proven successful and provides an extensive list of team teaching schools. A direct contact with any one of these school systems would be a source of tried and proven ideas and school plans. Also, each year the American Association of School Administrators produces a filmstrip based on the yearly Exhibition of School Architecture which is a fine source of current school construction information.

The schools of tomorrow will be drastically different in appearance as well as in organization, curriculum, and method. The schools of the future are going to utilize a great variety of grouping arrangements and other instructional techniques that will depend on and emphasize the need for maximum flexibility in space utilization. Schools designed today must emphasize flexibility in every way possible if they are to be useful educational centers for tomorrow.

10

Promising Innovations

A Unique Concept

The setting in which team teaching is first encountered often involves more educational innovations than just team teaching. Because of this, team teaching is sometimes thought to be a factor or part of some other educational development, such as the non-graded primary school, or the middle school, rather than a unique educational development.

There are a number of very promising curriculum and organizational innovations which are being explored or experimented with at present. (Note Breve 45.) These include multi-grading, non-grading, the middle school, individualized instruction, and flexible scheduling. Team teaching has been used in relation to these and other plans and in some situations has been a very necessary part of the plan and vice versa; however, the reader is asked to keep in mind that team teaching, although it often involves other innovations within its structure, is a unique educational movement in itself.

A host of exciting educational possibilities are available today. Some of these innovations that have been or could be utilized in a team

BREVE 45

Educational Innovations
Selected Listing

■ Aides—clerical, technical

■ Computer-assisted instruction (CAI)

■ Educational television (ETV)

■ Flexible scheduling

■ Grouping—ability,
                multi-grading,
                platoon,
                teachability,
                track systems.

■ Independent study

■ Individualized instruction

■ Micro-teaching

■ Middle school

■ Non-grading

■ Programed instruction

■ School-within-a-school

■ Teacher aides

■ Teaching machines

■ Teaching specialists—art,
                foreign language,
                music,
                physical education.
                remedial instruction, etc.

teaching structure are briefly described in this chapter. Because of space limitations no effort is made to present a detailed historical development or evaluation. However, a brief description of each innovation and its possible relationship to a team teaching situation is presented. For additional information about many of the new educational practices mentioned in this text the reader may wish to contact one of the federally supported Regional Educational Laboratories or Centers such as the Elk Grove Training and Development Center in Arlington Heights, Illinois, a suburb of Chicago. The primary purpose of the Center is to bridge the time lag between the creation of new innovations and the use of these practices in the classroom. Another Center that could be contacted is The Exemplary Center for Team Teaching of Weber County Schools, 1122 Washington Blvd., Ogden, Utah.

Middle School

The middle school is a school between the elementary school and the secondary school. It is a school for children between approximately 10 and 14 years of age. Usually it includes grades 5, 6, 7, and 8, but is sometimes two or more grades inclusive of grades 5 through 9. It should be noted that the "junior high school" meets this general definition and will probably be absorbed by the middle school movement.

A primary goal of the middle school is to further the self-development of its students in the areas of problem analysis, problem solving, study skills, social growth, emotional and physical development, and the several academic disciplines. The middle school is thought to be a place where children will be challenged to explore, develop, and build on their previous experience and training. It encompasses that developmental stage in which the student leaves childhood and enters early adolescence. Just as he is developing physically, other factors are also changing, and he needs a school setting in which a wide variety of educational experiences are available in many organizational patterns.

The curriculum for the middle school may be composed of social science, language arts, mathematics, science, and such concomitant areas as arts, crafts, home economics, music, physical education, and foreign languages. Classes may be organized along more traditional lines, but often the instructional staff is involved in team teaching activities. Ungraded units or non-grading is also often found in the middle school.

The middle school is normally housed in a separate building and draws students from several elementary schools. With a larger enrollment and more classes in the various subject areas, better and more specialized facilities are possible.

The middle school movement is a special effort to provide a more suitable environment where ten- to fourteen-year-old pupils can discover their abilities and learn with the guidance of teachers who understand their special needs. Also, it is an attempt to provide for flexibility and innovation. For this reason, middle schools frequently utilize team teaching and other features usually associated with team teaching.

Multi-grading

The one room, ungraded or perhaps multi-graded school was the first and most common of our traditional schools. During the late nineteenth century it gave way to the graded school. Today, because of its inflexibility, the graded school is being criticized and is giving way to other organizational plans. Multi-grading is one plan that has been proposed. Thus it would seem that innovative educators have gone full circle and come right back to the one-room schools, a few of which are still in operation in this country.

This "new" organizational plan, multi-grading, is as old as the one-room school but utilizes much up-to-date information about how children develop and learn. The mixing of younger and older children in the same classroom is thought by some educators to be good for both students and teachers. Younger students identify with the more mature children and an atmosphere for continuous learning is encouraged. The older students have opportunities to assist others and engage in independent study. The teacher is constantly reminded that he has a class of individuals and thus is more likely to teach each child rather than direct his lesson to the total group.

In the sense that teaching teams are sometimes organized on a vertical plan and therefore cross grade lines, a form of multi-grading is involved. We find this happening when a team is assigned students from two or more grade levels. The Dundee School of Greenwich, Connecticut assigns two or more grade levels to each teaching team and thus expands the grouping possibilities. On the secondary school level, because the focus of the teaching team is usually on a particular course or discipline rather than a certain grade level, students from several classes are often found in the same course.

Non-Graded School

The non-graded school is one in which traditional grade levels have been removed and children progress according to their ability. This program allows the adjustment of teaching and administrative procedures to meet the varying social, physical, and emotional needs of children on a more individual basis. Students are grouped together in classes which have no grade level designation.

The program promotes a philosophy in which failure and promotion are abandoned in favor of progress and continuous growth. Perhaps the basic structure of the non-graded program forces the classroom teacher to acknowledge the differences among children in a way that the graded school does not, while permitting each child to work at his own pace. The teacher has no grade level expectation against which to pace himself. His only obligation is to keep youngsters moving along as fast as they are capable of moving.

Development of the non-graded school movement has been promoted by growing dissatisfaction regarding promotional policies of the graded school, the belief that there is a need for a longer period of time for studying progress of pupils before making a decision on retention than permitted by the graded school, and a desire to eliminate the frustration and feeling of failure that accompanies non-promotion. The non-graded school attempts to accomplish these goals by providing several alternative vertical placements for all children at any time without the feeling of non-promotion or failure. In a non-graded school children are often assigned to groups that encompass a developmental range of two to three years, permitting a certain flexibility in moving a child from one group to the next.

Important components of the non-graded school are independent study, individualized instruction, and the use of various grouping patterns. Also, team teaching is often found in operation in non-graded situations.

Individualized and Independent Study

A one to one teacher-pupil ratio is generally agreed to provide the best education possible. But because of the pressure of numbers and cost it is also said to be impractical. However, within the framework of a non-graded, multi-graded, or team teaching organization a considerable amount of individualization is possible. Also, through the use of modern educational technology, new techniques which provide greater opportunity for individualized and independent study are being developed. Such techniques are needed because teachers must acknowledge and permit differences among students and attempt to work with these individual differences.

Much of what has been said about individualized instruction also applies to independent study. However, the concept of independent study goes further than just individualization for it requires that the

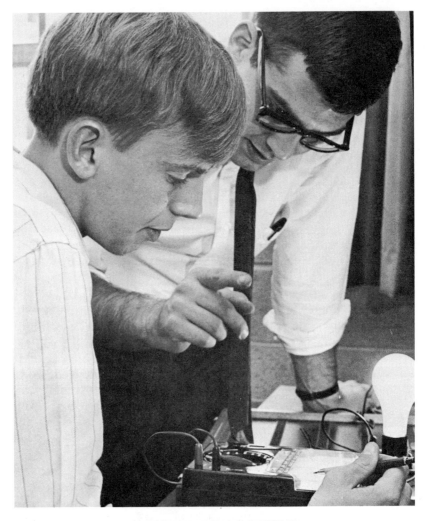

INDEPENDENT STUDY

student not only advance at his own rate through the use of various instructional aides but that he should be responsible for selecting his own objectives, planning much of his activity, and setting his own rate of progress. In its broadest sense, independent study can be interpreted as a means of allowing the student to proceed at his own pace in a problematic study which has been formulated, initiated, and planned with minimum direct supervision.

Individualized and independent study activities occur in a variety of settings. They can take place in the study hall, library, in specially designed study areas such as study carrels, or as a regular phase of the team teaching program.

Teaching Machines and Programed Instruction

A teaching machine is basically a device for presenting programed instruction. The features that are utilized in the process are small steps, active participation on the part of the student, immediate confirmation of the correctness of the response, and self-pacing.

Most teaching machines are designed to present a programed lesson to a student using a three part cycle: 1) the frame, 2) the response, and 3) the evaluation. The program is presented an item at a time in frames which allow the student to respond. They then provide feedback reinforcement, i.e. an immediate confirmation of the correctness of his response. The student then moves to the next item of information or is directed to review or study other material. Of special importance is the fact that the student progresses at his own rate. This complete process has sometimes been referred to as "automated teaching" since it requires less attention on the part of the teacher than a traditional teaching situation.

Generally speaking, there are two types of programed instruction: the constructed-response and the multiple-choice-response. It is important to remember that it is possible, and under certain circumstances considerably cheaper, to use programed instruction that does not require a teaching machine. There are many non-machine programed instruction materials available which are reported to be just as effective as those that make use of machine presentation.

Two well-known types of programed textbooks are the linear and the scrambled. A linear type is arranged in a series of minute steps through which the student proceeds one step at a time. A scrambled book is one in which each page is a unit. Programed instruction, with or without the use of teaching machines, is an important area of educational technology. Based upon sound learning theory and research, programed learning is a valuable aid in supplementing instruction and fulfilling enrichment and remedial objectives.

In a team teaching program the use of teaching machines and programed instruction lends itself completely to the concepts of individualized, independent, and small-group instruction. Teaching machines and programed instruction can be used with any subject from mathematics to industrial arts. This has been demonstrated not only in schools, but in the armed forces and industry. Such equipment and materials certainly have a place of importance in the Instructional Media Center and play an active role in the program of a good team teaching organization.

Flexible Scheduling

The importance of the master schedule of a school cannot be over-emphasized, especially in the introduction of an educational innovation such as team teaching. It sets forth in detail the "who, what, and where" of every class period of every school day. However, in many schools the schedule dominates the students and teachers it is supposed to serve. In a few schools, the schedule reflects fresh efforts to enliven and individualize instruction.

Computers have been proven capable of programing the most complex of school schedules. Schedules have been produced that take into account student and teacher preferences, innovations such as flexible scheduling and team teaching, and other specific circumstances without sacrificing efficiency of either staff or facilities. The Stanford School Scheduling System (SSSS) was a much used scheduling operation developed by the High School Flexible Scheduling and Curriculum Study at Stanford University in Palo Alto, California. This program now operates under the name Educational Coordinates.

The modular schedule is one type of flexible scheduling that is often used in connection with a team teaching organization. It schedules the school day into many "modules" of fifteen to twenty minutes in length rather than the traditional five- to seven-period school day. The team can schedule large- or small-group meetings, long discussion periods, short special project meetings, laboratory sessions, meetings with classes at different times during the day, and even omission of classes on some days to allow time for independent study. Traditional hour-long lectures can be presented by scheduling two or more modules together. Because of the difficulty in constructing these modular systems, computers are often used.

School-Within-A-School

The concept of a school-within-a-school is an approach to combating the problems of school size and the feeling of detachment often developed by pupils who attend very large schools. The total school is divided into two or more separate semi-independent schools, each with a separate administrative, teaching, and guidance staff, student body, and physical facilities. The students are usually divided randomly among the inter-schools. Each of the inter-schools has certain facilities of its own such as general laboratories and classrooms, but some facilities are centrally located and are shared by all schools. These usually include classrooms for the fine and technical arts, physical education, driver education, laboratories for advanced students, special music facilities, cafeteria, auditorium, and gymnasium. This arrangement permits the student to have most of his classes in the more informal atmosphere of a smaller school yet provides many of the advantages of a very large high school such as numerous course selections, staff specialization, and better physical facilities. Team teaching lends itself easily to the school-within-a-school concept and is frequently used in such an arrangement.

Computer Assisted Instruction

The last innovation to be considered is Computer Assisted Instruction (CAI). For some time the most prevalent use of data processing and computers in education was their application to administrative and school management requirements. Later the computer was used primarily as a teaching machine. In this capacity it was discovered that the computer could contribute to the teaching process by solving certain types of problems and locating up-to-date information. Recently, however, many schools have been using computers in classroom instruction as tools of instruction.

Such instruction is under the control of a computer. The basic elements involved include an electronic computer, an input station, *i.e.* a device by which the student can communicate with the computer, a retrieval station, *i.e.* a device through which the computer can relay information to the student, and a task that is suitable and can be programed for the computer.

Use of the computer for gaming and simulation is a valuable instructional technique. The student can experiment and gain experience, test alternative solutions, and observe answers to certain questions. Computer gaming and simulation of certain situations serve to extend the student beyond what could be accomplished in the traditional classroom setting. Although CAI is still basically experimental, great hopes are held for it. Certainly it will have a place of importance in the Instructional Media Center of every modern team teaching school.

part three

Team
Teaching
Patterns

11

Team Teaching Plans

Team teaching is still in the developmental stages. As the material in this chapter indicates, no one pattern or plan of organization has been universally accepted. Therefore, the views of the professional and nonprofessional personnel who are developing and administering today's team teaching programs are of great importance since they are the pioneers of this movement. The plans, procedures, and appraisals of selected teachers and administrators who are currently using some form of a team teaching organization were obtained by means of personal interviews and a mail questionnaire. Sixty-eight schools in seventeen states which were known to be operating innovative school organizations participated in this survey. This chapter presents a summation of certain information obtained in that survey. A selected list of schools which are using a form of team teaching is shown in Breve 46. This list is included to assist the student who may wish to contact one of the schools and also to illustrate how widespread the use of team teaching has become. It is interesting to note that several of the institutions claim a beginning date much earlier than 1957. However, it probably was not until after that date that the school began calling their instructional organization "team teaching."

BREVE 46

Team Teaching Schools
Selected List by State and Level

No.	Name	Location	Date Begun
		ELEMENTARY SCHOOLS	
1.	Bancroft Elementary	Walnut Creek, California	1968
2.	Dundee Elementary	Greenwich, Connecticut	1962
3.	University School		1963
	Indiana University	Bloomington, Indiana	
4.	Fairview Elementary	Auburn, Maine	1961
5.	Franklin Elementary	Lexington, Massachusetts	1957
6.	Evergreen Elementary		
	Birmingham Public School	Birmingham, Michigan	1965
7.	Lagrange Elementary	Toledo, Ohio	1967
8.	Fairfax Elementary	Mentor, Ohio	1967
9.	Sylvania-Whiteford		
	Sylvania Public Schools	Sylvania, Ohio	1968
10.	Oakleaf Elementary	Pittsburgh, Pennsylvania	1964
		MIDDLE AND JUNIOR HIGH SCHOOLS	
11.	Mabel E. O'Farrell		
	San Diego Unified Schools	San Diego, California	1959
12.	Alfred Plant Jr. H. S.	West Hartford, Connecticut	1965
13.	Jefferson Jr. H. S.	Decatur, Illinois	1963
14.	Barrington Middle School	Barrington, Illinois	1966
15.	Ben Davis Jr. H. S.	Indianapolis, Indiana	1966
16.	Meadowbrook Jr. H. S.	Newton Centre, Massachusetts	1962
17.	Howard B. Mattlin Jr. H. S.	Plainview, New York	1963
18.	Wahlquist Jr. H. S.	Ogden, Utah	1958
		SECONDARY SCHOOLS	
19.	Lincoln H. S.	Stockton, California	1963
20.	Arvada West H. S.	Arvada, Colorado	1963
21.	Lakeview H. S.	Decatur, Illinois	1960
22.	Homewood-Flossmoor H. S.	Flossmoor, Illinois	1965

(Con't.)

No.	Name	Location	Date Begun
23.	Rich Township H. S. East Campus	Park Forest, Illinois	1955
24.	Ridgewood H. S.	Norridge, Illinois	1960
25.	Evanston Twp. H. S.	Evanston, Illinois	1957
26.	W. P. Chrysler H. S.	New Castle, Indiana	1961
27.	Newton H. S.	Newton, Massachusetts	1958
28.	Franklin High School	Livonia, Michigan	1966
29.	Kent State University School	Kent, Ohio	1964
30.	Solon High School	Dolon, Ohio	1962
31.	Mayfield H. S.	Cleveland, Ohio	1960
32.	John Marshall H. S.	Portland, Oregon	1961
33.	Easton Area H. S.	Easton, Pennsylvania	1958
34.	Joel E. Ferris H. S.	Spokane, Washington	1963

COLLEGE AND UNIVERSITY

No.	Name	Location	Date Begun
35.	University of Hartford	Hartford, Connecticut	1966
36.	University of Southern Florida	Tampa, Florida	1966
37.	University of Maine	Orono, Maine	1961
38.	Boston University College of Basic Studies	Boston, Massachusetts	1949
39.	Macomb County Community College	Warren, Michigan	1966
40.	Monteith College of Wayne State University	Detroit, Michigan	1959

Elementary School

Much of the early interest in the team teaching movement centered around attempts to circumvent the obvious limitations of the self-contained classroom. On the elementary level this still remains an important reason for investigating team teaching. Frequently-mentioned goals of elementary school's efforts to reorganize are to secure better use of teacher strengths and talents, provide assistance to new teachers, relieve teachers of clerical and monitorial tasks, provide a broader curriculum for the children, arrange for greater flexibility in

BREVE 47

Elementary Designs

Selected List*

No.	Levels Involved	Curriculum	Organization		
			Pupils	Teachers	
3.	1st-6th grade	All subjects	By ability scores in subject area Judgment of team teachers	Cooperative Organization All teachers of a given grade level work as a team	
5.	Total school non-graded	All subjects	Three teams Alpha—6 & 7 yr. old Beta—8 & 9 yr. old Omega—10 & 11 yr. old Instructional groups planned to meet pupil needs	Team leaders responsible for grouping & instruction Senior teacher specialist in curriculum- assists all teachers Teachers Teacher Aides	

	Grade	Subjects	Grouping	Staff
6.	Kg.-6th grade	All subjects	By ability scores in Language Arts & Math	Team leader-Administrator Senior teacher Curriculum Leader Special Teachers- Social Studies & Science Several teachers
7.	2nd grade	All subjects	By ability in reading and 1st grade teacher's judgment	Project Coordinator 2 team teachers-instructional 3 student teachers 2 part-time aides (college sophomores) 2 part-time participants (college juniors)
9.	1st-6th grades	All subjects	By grade, achievement, test scores, & teacher judgment	Cooperative Leadership 2 regular teachers 2 team assistants (student teachers)

*Schools may be identified by number. Refer to Breve 46.

meeting the individual needs of students, improve physical facility utilization, and obtain greater faculty involvement. Breve 47 shows some of the instructional organizations that have been developed in an effort to accomplish these goals in the elementary school.

Assignment of children to a team on the elementary level is most often on the basis of grade level or scores on standardized achievement tests. In non-graded organizations, criteria that are sometimes used are the child's age and teacher judgment. Heterogeneous grouping is usually used in assigning students to homeroom situations and certain subjects such as social studies, physical education, and other subjects that emphasize social understanding and development.

In elementary schools it is a common practice to assign responsibility for all of the subjects offered in a particular grade to a team since children are often assigned to the team by grade level. Specialists are used, however, in certain subject areas, such as music, art, and physical education. This technique not only provides for student exposure to more teachers but frees the regular team members to plan together, develop team policy, and study.

Although it is possible to establish a teaching team organization which involves only one grade level or a particular subject, few of the elementary schools surveyed did so. Most had involved the entire school and organized several teams on a grade, ability level, or age basis.

The hierarchical organizational pattern seemed to be the most prevalent design on the elementary level. The cooperative approach was the next most frequently used. Only about one-third of the elementary schools surveyed reported the use of aides or teacher assistants as a part of the team organization.

The Middle School and Junior High School

Educational literature makes a distinction between the middle school and the junior high school by defining the latter as encompassing grades 7, 8, and 9 while the middle school includes 5, 6, 7, and 8. Actual practice deviates from these recommendations, however, to the extent that the names have little meaning in terms of the exact grades included in a particular school with one or the other title. Generally speaking, both terms simply mean that the organization involves some combination of the middle and upper elementary grades.

Traditionally, in the instructional organization of the upper elementary grades, the use of departmentalized plans involving teacher specialists has always been more common than on the primary or middle grade levels. But these programs still center around the

BREVE 48

Middle and Junior High Designs
Selected list*

Levels No. Involved	Curriculum	Pupils	Teachers
		Organization	
11. 7-9th grades	All subjects except Industrial Arts & Foreign Language	No difference in assignment to team & to conventional class.	Team Leader responsible for leadership & operation of team Team Member works with team leader Teacher Assistant student enrolled in a teacher training program, certified.
12. 7-8th grades	All academic subjects plus Music and Art	By grade, I.Q., and Performance in subject	Team Leader Specialists (Art, Music, Counselor) Teachers Student Teachers (Central Connecticut State College)
13. 7-8th grades	Math, Science English, Social Studies, Home Economics, & Industrial Arts	By grade Ability scores in subjects	Cooperative Organization 2-3 team members in each department & grade level One teacher does large group lectures All teachers plan large & small group presentations

*Schools may be identified by number. Refer to Breve 46.

Organization

No.	Levels Involved	Curriculum	Pupils	Teachers
14.	6, 7, 8th grades (called 1st, 2nd, and 3rd year students)	All subjects	1st year (6th) by grade. 2nd (7th) and 3rd (8th) year by subject	1st year—Cooperative Organization: each member assumes major academic area planning and/or instruction 2nd & 3rd—Department Teams: each team member assumes lead responsibility for his specialized area
15.	7-9th grades	All subjects	By subject	Cooperative Organization Organized by Academic Disciplines
17.	7-9th grades	All subjects	By grade By subject	One team leader for all 3 teams, grades 7, 8, & 9 Teachers are organized into grade level sub-teams by subject (e.g. three teachers of Math for grade 7) No team leaders in sub-teams
18.	7-9th grades	Language Arts, Social Studies, Instrumental Music, Vocal Music, Science, Art, & Math	By grade By ability scores in Math	Cooperative Organization Leadership emerges as curriculum involves a teacher's specialty Teams consist of from 2-7 members chosen according to their interest in a given subject area

concept of one teacher planning and controlling a class. Because of this, the reasons middle and junior high schools give for experimenting with team teaching organization are similar to those mentioned for the elementary school.

Of the middle or junior high schools surveyed, many used the cooperative organizational design. In both the hierarchical and cooperative plans, the children were most frequently assigned to the team on a grade level basis with achievement on standardized test and I. Q. scores sometimes taken into account. Usually the entire school was involved in the team teaching organization but occasionally certain subjects such as industrial arts or foreign languages were not included. Breve 48 shows more detailed information in regard to various instructional organizations being used on the middle and junior high school levels.

Secondary School

The subject-centered organization used by most high schools, like the departmentalized upper elementary grade organization, has done much to bring a more knowledgeable teacher before the students; however, the subject-centered organization still must rely largely on one teacher's ability to plan and control instruction. For this and other reasons many high school faculties are experimenting with instructional organizations which can be classified as team teaching.

Twenty-eight high schools in twelve states were contacted as part of the author's team teaching survey. Both the traditional four-year high school (9-12) and the senior high school (10-12) are represented. Information regarding this selected group of participating high schools is shown in Breve 49.

The majority of the high schools reported using a cooperative organizational design. Student teachers and aides were found on both the hierarchical and cooperative teams. Cooperative designs were often described as peer relationships since the team members worked as equals in a voluntary arrangement. Some schools reported having team leaders for only the larger teams.

Although half of the high schools indicated that they assigned students to teams by grade level, the subject involved was also mentioned as an assignment criteria by two-thirds of the group. Ability scores, a very important assignment criteria on the elementary level, were rarely mentioned on the secondary level. The computer was used to make student assignments in some high schools.

Whereas most elementary and middle or junior high schools stated that the teaching teams were responsible for the total curriculum for

Secondary Designs
Selected List*

| | Levels | Organization | | | |
| No. | Involved | Curriculum | Pupils | Teachers | |

No.	Levels Involved	Curriculum	Pupils	Teachers
21.	9-12th grades	All	By subject with interdisciplinary teams for under-achievers and Humanities	Cooperative Organization Each team responsible for entire organization & function of subject Large & Small group instruction Duties of Team member decided by team
22.	9-12th grades Four levels Honors Advanced Intermediate Basic	All, except P.E. & Foreign Language	By subject	2-8 member teams Division of presentation & preparation

25.	9-12th grades	Combined Studies (Core program—Eng. Soc. St.), Home Economics, Driver Ed., Girl's P. E., Industrial Education, and Speech Arts (Title III Project, ESEA '65)	By grade By subject	Decided by departments Each department has complete autonomy as to organization & administration
28.	10-12th grades	Art, Business Education, Home Economics, Industrial Education, Math, Science, & Social Studies, English	By subject as assigned at random by computer.	All members volunteer to be involved in Team Teaching. They volunteered to participate with other specific teachers on that specific team
29.	(1964) Grade 12	Humanities (Man as expressed in literature, art and music)	Elective Grade 12 65 students	1 English 1 Music 1 Art
	(1965) Grade 11	American Studies (Amer. Hist., Amer. Lit., related art and music)	All Grade 11 100 students	1 Social Study 1 English 1 Music 1 Art

* Schools may be identified by number. Refer to Breve 46.

BREVE 49

(Con't.)

No.	Levels Involved	Organization		
		Curriculum	Pupils	Teachers
29. (Con't.)	(1966) Grade 10	World Studies (World Hist., World Lit., related art and music)	All Grade 10 100 students	1-1/2 English 1 Social Study Art & Music part time
	(1967) Grade 12	Communications & Understanding (Prob. of Democracy-Senior English)	Elective 56 students	1 English 1 Social Study
	(1967) Grade 11 (2 yr. prog.)	Chemistry-Physics (PSSC Physics & CHEMS Chemistry)	Elective with permission of instructors. 24 students	1 Physics 1 Chemistry
34.	9-12th grade	All areas also have inter-discipline teams, Guidance teams	By subject	Both vertical & horizontal organization Team leader Two team teachers One paraprofessional

BREVE 50

College and University Designs

Selected Listing*

Organization

No.	Levels Involved	Curriculum	Pupils	Teachers
35.	Sophomore	Education students (Introduction to Education)	Required for Education majors—elective for others	Elementary Education Specialist Secondary Education Specialist Social Psychologist Urban Psychologist Administrator Two graduate Assistants
36.	Last half of under graduate degree (Approximately two years)	Program for preparation of elementary teachers	Program elected by student	Inter-disciplinary team

*Schools may be identified by number. Refer to Breve 46.

Organization

No.	Levels Involved	Curriculum	Pupils	Teachers
37.	Sophomores Juniors Seniors	Basic course work in education	Required of all Education Majors	Cooperative Organization Team Leader elected each year's series as sec. to team
38.	Freshmen & Sophomores	Entire program	Random selection	Cooperative Organization
39.	Freshmen	Basic Education	American College Test Scores	Team Communications Instructor Natural Science Instructor Social Science Instructor Humanities Instructor Counselor Instructors integrate subject matter & coordinate testing, etc.

a particular grade level, few of the high schools indicated this arrangement. The majority of the high school teaching teams were concerned with a subject arrangement involving only one, two, or three subjects. The subjects most frequently mentioned as being team taught were English, social studies, and science (biology in most cases), or some combination of these.

Higher Education

Colleges and universities are experimenting with the team teaching concept. This development reinforces the theory that team teaching is applicable at all grade levels and in all areas of the curriculum. Breve 50 illustrates how the teachers, students, and curriculum are involved in team teaching organizations at certain institutions of higher education.

The reasons mentioned for entering a team teaching arrangement on the college level were very similar to those usually mentioned on the elementary and secondary levels. They included personalized instruction, flexibility of time, and focus on students' needs.

12

Critique

A critique would normally be a personal evaluation or critical discussion. However, rather than limit this critique to the author's conclusions, information provided by the respondents to the author's "team teaching" questionnaire will be presented. Each reader is encouraged to compile his own team teaching "critique."

Only schools that were reported in the professional journals, newsletters, or other reports to be using team teaching were contacted. Of the schools receiving questionnaires only four reported that they had "dropped" team teaching once they tried it. Also, of the elementary schools surveyed, one half reported that they had adopted a team teaching organization sometime before 1965. This would seem to indicate that most schools that adopt a team teaching organization find it accomplishes the goals set for it. Comments reported and shown in Breve 51 seem to suggest this, also.

Problems

There are far fewer responses to the question, "What should be considered the greatest problems in team teaching?" than to the

BREVE 51

Representative Comments
Selected List*

ELEMENTARY DESIGNS

No.	Benefits	Problems
5.	Meeting children's individual needs. Continuous evaluation by teachers of self, students, and curriculum.	Time to do the job teachers demand of themselves
6.	Flexibility in meeting needs of individual pupils. Continual teacher In-service (planned and incidental) Possibility of using best in each teacher	Development of materials for multi-subgroups. Evaluative tools not available to use in assessing students. Change factor even for those teachers enthused about team teaching
7.	Provide small group instruction. Individual needs better met	Staff communication & relationships
8.	Utilizes space & teacher's time to best advantage. Creates situations ranging from individualized instruction to large group instruction. Opportunities for remedial & enrichment work	Personality conflicts

*Schools may be identified by number. Refer to Breve 46.

(Con't)

No.	Benefits	Problems
	Child responds to more than one teacher	
	Provides self-evaluation & team evaluation	

MIDDLE AND JUNIOR HIGH SCHOOL DESIGNS

No.	Benefits	Problems
12.	Cooperative Planning Distribution of work Field trip arrangement	Use of space in an old (1925) building
15.	Allows a pooling & sharing of ideas Allows constructive professional criticism Allows teaching in areas of specialized strengths Encourages better preparation Furnishes beginning teachers valuable in-service experience	Developing real teamwork rather than cooperative teaching Adequate time for planning Rapport of members

SECONDARY DESIGNS

No.	Benefits	Problems
19.	Able to break group into small sections Better use of staff time & talent More than one approach for students to hear in the various subject areas More & better preparation by teachers	Having compatable team members Using time wisely Coordinating small groups to go along with lecture

(Con't)

No.	Benefits	Problems
25.	Instill in young people a sense of self-directiveness in preparing for their educational training Opportunity for efficient & effective staff utilization	Acquiring, training, and retraining teachers who can teach in such a situation Adequate & competent team staff members difficult to come by
28.	Capitalization of the strengths & weaknesses of each teacher Utilization of time Students exposed to excellent teachers Close working unity between teachers	Convincing more teachers that Team Teaching is beneficial to them & to students—especially teachers who like to "hide" behind closed doors of their classrooms
29.	Allows for meaningful multi-discipline approach in depth. Helps to make both history & English relevant to needs of student. Allows for small interest group & inter-action sections. Allows students to be exposed to skills of all teachers. Class also becomes more meaningful and interesting. Related social problems & communication skills into one program using talents of two teachers. Saving of time where same topic is taught in	Using small group discussion technique advantages vs lecture methods Developing an ever-changing curriculum during the normal school year or the program is interest-centered. Re-training of faculty to get maximum benefits out of small group discussion. Developing program "on the spot"—using team teaching possibilities to fill advantage Insufficient time in schedule-planning

(Con't)

No.	Benefits	Problems
	both chemistry & physics. Ability group in classroom.	More economical use of time with schedule of integration.

COLLEGE AND UNIVERSITY DESIGNS

No.	Benefits	Problems
36.	Personalized instruction Flexible use of time Focus on children and assume the professor's a subject matter buff Much planning & discussing how we are doing with students as individuals Vast reduction of over-lapping and repetition Escape from coursism	Breaking allegiance to a course
37.	Stimulating each other produces continuing growth in ourselves & in courses we teach All usual benefits, such as flexible grouping, etc.	Finding people who are open enough and secure enough to try (at college level)
40.	Students, "average" when admitted, score 70-80th percentile in the three area portions of the Graduate Record Exam Lower drop-out rate 60-80% of graduates go on to graduate and professional schools	Faculty experience difficulty in disciplining themselves to this interdisciplinary approach—harder to keep up with their own disciplines

question, "What are its benefits?" The problem mentioned most frequently was that of securing teachers who can work together cooperatively. Mixing people of different teaching styles and personalities can
result in conflicts. At all levels, finding teachers who can deal with
one another and the problems of the classroom in a professional manner is apparently difficult.

Another frequently mentioned difficulty of the team approach was
finding time to schedule group activities, plan instructional and material development, and conduct team study. This problem was mentioned at all levels—elementary, middle and junior high, secondary,
and university. The difficulty of scheduling physical facilities was also
mentioned by the elementary and middle-junior high schools.

Dread of the unfamiliar, teacher insecurity, and lack of understanding of the team teaching concept are apparently obstacles to beginning
a team organization. On the secondary and college level the fact that
the team approach tends to restrict the individual teacher's freedom of
action was often mentioned, also.

Contradiction did arise on one item. Some respondents reported that
team teaching increased teacher involvement with students; however,
others stated that there was danger of pupil detachment and that
teachers did not know the students as well.

Benefits

Each respondent was asked to state "the greatest benefit that re-
sulted from team teaching." The most frequently mentioned advantage
dealt with the "built-in" in-service education opportunities for teachers. Because teachers plan together, share information and ideas, and
help one another solve problems, their professional competency is
generally improved. The group as a whole seems capable of accomplishing more than the individuals could working independently.
According to the respondents, staff members in a team organization
instruct, stimulate, and encourage each other so that each person does
his very best. Such activity produces a general improvement in the
instructional program.

An advantage to the student that was frequently mentioned is that
the team approach provides enough flexibility to better meet the
varying needs of the different school populations. Greater attention
can be paid to individual differences because there is more opportunity to group pupils in areas or courses according to their needs and
interests.

Another point made about grouping was the improved control of pupil-staff ratio provided by the use of large-, medium-, and small-group arrangements in ways not possible in the isolated classroom. Also, grouping allows more effective use of the time and professional talents of the staff members.

Greater opportunity for good teachers to meet with all students was mentioned by many respondents. The converse is also true—the team approach can neutralize the effect of the poor teacher.

Some schools claimed that using a team approach to instruction provides new educative experiences for the students and generally brings about a more balanced curriculum. It also allows students to work across grade and subject lines with subject matter specialists.

The following are points mentioned only by a few respondents: team teaching seems to produce a lower dropout rate; pupils become more independent; there is less overlap in schoolwork, homework, and field trip experiences; teachers are relieved of routine tasks through the use of aides; and a team teaching arrangement offers a greater opportunity to give dignity and prestige to the profession.

The last point mentioned above regarding professional prestige is a very important one even though it was mentioned only occasionally by the respondents. The team teaching idea, when completely activated, calls for relieving the professional staff of non-instructional duties so that their time, and expensive time it is today, too, can be devoted to teaching and those tasks closely related to it. The introduction of non-certified personnel into the classroom serves to clearly identify the certified individual as a person who has acquired certain skills and met certain standards. Then too, the hierarchy organization requires teachers of various levels of competence ranging from the provisional teacher to the executive teacher. There is no doubt that salaries will eventually be adjusted to this arrangement and this will enable the highly educated, excellent teacher to remain in the class-room with dignity.

Versatility

Team teaching has caught the fancy of groups in almost every phase of education. Reports have been received from religious groups who train converts stating that they are using a team organization in their teaching. The special education classes in the Weber County School District, Ogden, Utah, have been integrated with the regular classes in the elementary school and the teachers are participating as part of the teacher-team assigned to that school. In training young people for various sports the team approach has long been used. The coach of a football team will very often have several assistants who work with him forming a coaching-training team.

From sports to religion, in all subject areas, and at every educational level from nursery school through the university, word has come that team teaching was tried and found to accomplish the goals set for it. Is it the instructional organization of the future?

for further study

Selected
References

In an effort to limit this bibliography and yet present current thinking on the subject, only references that have a copyright date of 1962 or later were considered for inclusion unless they were specifically mentioned in the text. If the reader wishes information on the preceding years, the author recommends the annual reports of the National Association of Secondary School Principals, National Education Association, Commission on the Experimental Study of the Utilization of the Staff in the Secondary School:

1958: "New Horizons in Staff Utilization," Vol. 42, No. 234.
1959: "Exploring Improved Teaching Patterns: Second Report on Staff Utilization," Vol. 43, No. 24.
1960: "Progressing Toward Better Schools: Third Report on Staff Utilization Studies," Vol. 44, No. 252.
1961: "Seeking Improved Learning Opportunities: Fourth Report on Staff Utilization Studies," Vol. 45, No. 261.

Suggested References—Chapter 1

Alonso, Braulio, "Time to Teach," Address 1968 Ohio Elementary School Principals Professional Conference, Columbus, Ohio (October, 1968).

Anderson, Robert H., "Team Teaching," *NEA Journal*, L (March, 1961), 52.

Boehm, E. M., "Duty-free Lunch Time," *Instructor*, LXXI (October, 1961), 32.

Brownell, John A. and Harris A. Taylor, "Theoretical Perspectives for Teaching Teams," *Phi Delta Kappan*, XLIII (January, 1962), p. 157.

Dean, Stuart E. and Clinette F. Witherspoon, "Team Teaching in the Elementary School," *Education Briefs*, OE-23022. Washington, D.C.: U.S. Department of Health, Education, and Welfare (January, 1962).

Elliot, Richard W., "Team Teaching: Effective In-service Training," *American School Board Journal*, CXLIV (February, 1962), 19.

Flanagan, John C., "Functional Education for the '70's," *Phi Delta Kappan*, XLIX (September, 1967), 28.

Freeman, Stanley L., *Third Annual Report to the Ford Foundation on Team Teaching in Maine 1963-1964*, Orono, Maine: The University of Maine (February, 1965).

Gambold, Willard J., "The Modern Teacher and New Media of Instruction," *Education*, LXXXIII (October, 1962), 67.

Georgiades, William, "Team Teaching: A New Star, Not a Meteor," *NEA Journal*, LVI (April, 1967), p. 14.

Hayes, Charles H., "Team Teaching in Culturally Deprived Areas," *The National Elementary Principal*, XLIV (January, 1965), 60.

Ingram, J. F., "Time for Team Teaching," *American Vocational Journal*, XLII (February, 1967), 20.

Landers, J. and C. Mercurio, "Improving Curriculum and Instruction for the Disadvantaged Minorities; Team Teaching," *Journal of Negro Education*, XXXIV (Summer, 1965), 362.

Mitchell, Wanda B., "Why Try Team Teaching?" *NASSP Bulletin*, LXVI (January, 1962), 11.

Shaplin, Judson T. and Henry F. Olds, Jr. (Eds.), *Team Teaching*, New York, N.Y.: Harper and Row, Publishers, 1964.

Stevens, J. C., "More Time for Teaching," *National Association of Secondary School Principal's Bulletin*, XLVI (December, 1962), 54.

Wiles, Kimball, "Education of Adolescents: 1985," *Educational Leadership*, XVII (May, 1960), 480.

Suggested References—Chapter 2

Beggs, David W., *Team Teaching; Bold New Venture*. Indianapolis, Indiana: Unified College Press Incorporated, 1964.

Heller, Melvin P. and Elizabeth Belford, "Team Teaching and Staff Utilization in Ridgewood H. S.," *NASSP Bulletin*, XLVI (January, 1962), 105.

Michael, Lloyd, "Team Teaching," *NASSP Bulletin*, XLVII (May, 1963), 36.

Nimicht, Glendon P., "A Second Look at Team Teaching," *NASSP Bulletin*, XLVI (December, 1962), 64.

Olson, Carl, "We Call It 'Team Teaching'—But Is It Really That?" *Grade Teacher*, LXXXIII (October, 1965), p. 842.

Singer, Ira, "Survey of Staff Utilization Practices in Six States," *NASSP Bulletin*, XLVI (January, 1962), 1.

Suggested References—Chapter 3

Brown, Charles I., "Make It a Team Teaching Venture," *The Clearing House*, XXXVII (February, 1963), 340.

Brownell, John A. and Harris A. Taylor, "Theoretical Perspectives for Teaching Teams," *Phi Delta Kappan*, XLIII (January, 1962), 150.

Davis, D. A., "Tennville Teacher Aide Experiment," *Journal of Teacher Education*, XIII (June, 1962), 189.

"Hierarchy in Team Teaching," *NASSP Bulletin*, XLVI (December, 1962), 59.

"How Aides Can Improve A Physical Education Program," *School Management*, VI (December, 1962), 54.

"Lay Reader Program in Review," *National Association of Secondary School Principal's Bulletin*, XLVI (January, 1962), 20.

Marks, Merle B., "The Assistant Teacher," *NASSP Bulletin*, (March, 1964), 56.

Ship, Mary D., "Teacher Aides in Large School Systems," *National Education Association Circular*, (April, 1967), 1.

Stafford, C., "Teacher Time Utilization With Teacher Aides," *Journal of Educational Research*, LVI (October, 1962), 82.

Thomson, S. D., "Emerging Role of the Teacher Aide," *Clearing House*, XXXVII (February, 1963), 326.

Turney, D. T., "Secretarial Help for Classroom Teachers," *Educational Digest*, XXVII (December, 1962), 24.

Suggested References—Chapter 4

Anderson, Edward J., "Crackling Excitement in School Corridors: How We Made the Change-over," *Life Magazine*, LIV (March 22, 1963), 78.

Bair, Medill, *Team Teaching in Action*. Boston, Mass: Houghton Mifflin Company, Inc., 1964.

Clement, Stanley L., "More Time for Teaching," *NASSP Bulletin*, XLVI (December, 1962), 54.

Davis, Harold S., *How to Organize an Effective Team Teaching Program*. Englewood Cliffs, New Jersey: Prentice-Hall, Inc., 1966.

Douglass, H. R., *Modern Administration of Secondary Schools*. Boston, Mass.: Ginn and Co., 1963.

Dundee Team Teaching Project, A Research Report Prepared by the Institute of Field Studies, Teachers College, Columbia University, New York, 1965.

Hoopes, Ned E., "The Training Process for Team Teaching," *The Journal of Teacher Education*, XIV (June, 1963), 177.

Inviolata, Sister Ms, "How We Organized for Team Teaching," *Catholic School Journal*, LXV (May, 1965), 149.

Lobb, M. Delbert, *Practical Aspects of Team Teaching*. San Francisco, California: Fearon Publishers, 1964.

Shumsky, Abraham and Ross Mukarji, "From Research Idea to Classroom Practice," *Elementary School Journal*, LXIII (November, 1963).

Trump, J. Lloyd, "Problems Faced in Organizing a School Differently," *American School Board Journal*, CXLVII (November, 1963), 70.

Suggested References—Chapter 5

"Administrative Developments Discussion Groups: Team Teaching," *NASSP Bulletin*, XLVI (October, 1962), 53.

Barnard, Chester I., *The Functions of the Executive*. Cambridge, Mass.: Harvard University Press, 1938.

Fox, Willard and Alfred Schwartz, *Managerial Guide for School Principals*. Columbus, Ohio: Charles E. Merrill Publishing Co., 1965.

Griffiths, Daniel E., *Behavioral Science and Educational Administration,* 1964 Yearbook of the National Society for the Study of Education, Chicago, Illinois: The University of Chicago Press, 1964.

King, Arthur R., Jr., "Planning for Team Teaching, The Human Considerations," *California Journal of Secondary Education,* XXXVII (October, 1962), 362.

National Society for the Study of Education, *Behavioral Science and Educational Administration.* Chicago, Illinois: University of Chicago Press, 1964.

"Planning for Team Teaching," *Education,* LXXXV (February, 1965), 333-36.

Rohrer, Hibler and Replogle, *Managers for Tomorrow.* New American Library, New York, N.Y., 1965.

Suggested References—Chapter 6

Congreve, Willard J., "Toward Independent Learning," *North Central Association Quarterly,* XXXVII (Spring, 1963), 16.

"Design for Team Teaching," *The Instructor,* (May, 1968), 65.

Drummond, Harold D., "Team Teaching: An Assessment," *Educational Leadership,* XIX (December, 1961), 160.

Durrell, Donald O., "Team Learning," *Grade Teacher,* LXXVII (June, 1960), 20.

Peterson, Carl H., "Is Team Teaching for Your Schools?" *American School Board Journal,* CXLIV (February, 1962), 11.

Trump, J. Lloyd, "Flexible Scheduling: Fad or Fundamental?" *Phi Delta Kappan,* XLIV (May, 1963), 367.

Suggested References—Chapter 7

Bernhardt, Karl L., *Discipline and Child Guidance.* New York, N.Y.: McGraw-Hill Book Company, 1964.

Hall, Nason E., Jr., "Saving the Trouble-Prone," *NEA Journal,* (April, 1965), 26.

Kvaraceus, William C., "Deviancy or Dry Rot in the Classroom?" *Educational Leadership,* XXIV (April, 1967), 585.

Lambert, Philip, "Team Teaching for the Elementary School," *Educational Leadership,* XVIII (November, 1960), 85.

Marsh, Robert, "Team Teaching: New Concept?" *Clearing House,* XXXV (April, 1961), 496.

Schain, Robert L., and Murray Polner, *Using Effective Discipline for Better Class Control.* New York, N.Y.: Teachers Practical Press, Inc., 1964.

Webster, Staten W., *Discipline in the Classroom*. Chicago, Illinois: Chandles Publishing Company, 1968.

Suggested References—Chapter 8

Becker, Harry A., "Team Teaching," *Instructor*, LXXI (June, 1962), 43.
Dale, Edgar, *Audio-Visual Methods in Teaching*. Revised Edition. New York, N.Y.: The Dryden Press, Inc., 1954.
Davis, Harold S., "Illuminate the Lecture!" *Educational Screen and Audio-visual Guide*, XLIV (March, 1965), 20.
Echols, Dan, "The Making of a Media Center," *Audio-Visual Instruction*, XII (October, 1967), 799.
Farrar, W. W., "Sequence of Events," *Audio-Visual Instruction*, X (April, 1965), 299.
Morlan, John E., "Think Twice About Team Teaching," *Instructor*, LXXIII (September, 1963), 65.
Walker, Wally, "Team Teaching: Pros and Cons," *CTA Journal*, LVIII (April, 1962), 17.

Suggested References—Chapter 9

Coody, B. E. and W. S. Sandefur, "Designing Schools for Variability," *Educational Leadership*, XXIV (March, 1967), 505.
Haeckel, Lester C., "Facilities for Elementary Team Teaching," *American School Board Journal*, LXLVI (January, 1963), 27.
Laline, Arthur W., "Elementary Schools Designed for Team Teaching," *Audio-Visual Instructor*, VII (October, 1962), 540.
Moore, J. D., "Berwyn, Pennsylvania, Junior High Designed for Learning," *American School Board Journal*, CLII (April, 1966), 16.
Pratt, H. M., "Space, a Plan to Meet Children's Needs," *Instructor*, LVI (January, 1967), 19.
Woolbridge, James H. and Frank E. Mayer, "Building for Team Teaching," *Ohio Schools*, Vol. XL (May 5, 1962), 15.

Suggested References—Chapter 10

Bethune, Paul and Burt Kaufman, "Nova High—Space Age School," *Phi Delta Kappan*, XLVI (September, 1964), 9.
Brian, Sister M., "TV Demands a Teaching Team," *Catholic School Journal*, LXV (May, 1965), 38.
Formsma, Jay W., "A New High School With A New Look," *North Central Association Quarterly*, XXXVII (Spring, 1963), 293.

Gemma, Sister Mary, "Why Flexibility is our Answer," *Catholic School Journal*, LXV (April, 1965), 47.
Grooms, Ann, *Perspectives on the Middle School*. Columbus: Ohio: Charles E. Merrill Publishing Co., 1967.
Howard, Eugene R., and Roger W. Bardwell, *How to Organize a Non-Graded School*. Englewood Cliffs, New Jersey: Prentice-Hall, Inc., 1966.
Spring, Bernard P., "Plug-In Schools: Next Step in Educational Design?" *Architectural Forum*, CIXX (August, 1963), 68.
Tewksbury, John L., *Nongrading in the Elementary School*. Columbus, Ohio: Charles E. Merrill Publishing Co., 1967.

Suggested References—Chapter 11

Baynham, D., "Selected Staff Utilization Projects in California, Georgia, Colorado, Illinois, Michigan, and New York," *National Association of Secondary School Principal's Bulletin*, XLVI (January, 1962), 14.
Cerrl, Lawrence, "Team Teaching: How It Works in Niskayuna," *Scholastic Teacher*, LXXXVIII (March 25, 1966), 298.
Fischler, Abraham S., "The Use of Team Teaching in the Elementary School," *School Science and Math*, LXII (April, 1962), 287.
Gross, Calvin E., "Team Teaching in Pittsburgh," *Education Digest*, XXVIII (November, 1962), 12.
Harrison, William J., "Team Teaching at Muskegon, Michigan, Sr. H. S.," *NASSP Bulletin*, XLVI (January, 1962), 239.
Hathaway, Larry, "Team Teaching in Illinois H. S.," *American Teacher*, XLVI (April, 1962), 11.
Langer, Howard J., "Team Teaching at Dundee," *Scholastic Teacher*, LXXXII, (February 27, 1963) 5T.
Lonsdale, Bernard J., "Television and Team Teaching in California Elementary Schools," *California Journal of Elementary Education*, XXXI (November, 1962), 74.
Peterson, Carl H., "Team Teaching in the High School," *Education*, LXXXV (February, 1965), 342.
"Team Teaching and Flexible Grouping in the Junior High School Social Studies," *Journal of Experimental Education*, 34 (Fall, 1965), 20-32.

Suggested References—Chapter 12

Battrick, D. H., "How Do Team Teaching and Other Staff Utilization Practices Fit Into the Instructional Program of a Junior High School?" *NASSP Bulletin*, XLVI (October, 1962), 13.
Blake, Roy F., "Small Group Research and Cooperative Teaching Problems," *National Elementary Principal*, XLIII (February, 1964), 31.

Borg, W. R. and L. R. Brite, "Teacher's Perceptions of Team Teaching," *California Journal of Educational Research*, XVIII (March, 1967), 71.

Carlin, Philip M., "A Current Appraisal of Team Teaching," *Education*, LXXXV (February, 1965), 348.

Corrigan, Dean and Robert Hynes, "What Have We Learned From Team Teaching?," *Social Education*, XXVIII (April, 1964), 205.

Davis, Russell C., "Teacher Assessment of Team Teaching," *Science Teacher*, XXXIII (December, 1966), 38.

Kelly, E. T., "Why Team Teaching Fails," *Instructor*, LXXVI (April, 1967), 25.

Lambert, Philip, "Team Teaching for Today's World," *Teachers College Record*, LXIV (March, 1963), 480.

Pitruzzello, Philip R., "A Report on Team Teaching," *Clearing House*, XXXVI (February, 1962), 333.

Polos, Nicholas C., "Team Teaching: Past, Present, and Future," *Clearing House*, XXXIX (April, 1965), 456.

Index

and individual instruction, 77
initial design, 44
initiating, 42
limitations, 9, 11
main problem of, 138
and multi-grading, 108
and non-grading, 109
and non-professional duties, 139
non-professional staff, 35
and organization, 17
and physical facilities, 93, 94, 95
and planning, 43, 45
problems, 134-37
professional staff, 27
and programed instruction, 111
reasons for, 6
research and instruction unit, 22
and routines, 76
and school records, 75

schools, 118-19
and school-within-a-school idea, 113
and student assignment, 49
and students, 71
successful, 11, 51, 55, 66
tailor-made approach to, 42
and teacher behavior, 25
and teaching machines, 111
and training, 46
vertical organization, 16, 21, 108
Technical aide, 34, 35, 36
Technology, 84, 109
Tests, 64, 125
Training, 37, 46
Trump, J. Lloyd, 18

Universities, 129-30, 131, 137

Weber County School District, 139
Witherspoon, Clinette F., 13